Cozy Vegan is the ultimate kitchen companion for those wanting to explore a plant-based lifestyle, feel incredible, and not sacrifice the delicious foods they love. With colorful, balanced meals and vegan twists on your favorite comfort foods, home cook and Instagram foodie Liz Douglas, creator of @glowdiaries___, is here to show you how effortless vegan cooking can be.

In this cookbook, you'll find easy and exciting breakfast recipes to start your day, such as the make-ahead Choc Chia Mousse or savory Pumpkin Seed Scramble for a filling weekend brunch. If you're new to vegan cooking, Liz has you covered with basic pantry-staple recipes for cream, cheese, eggs, spreads, and more that you can make at home to save money. When it comes to mains, you won't be left hungry with hearty meals like Classic Beef Lasagna, creamy Butter Chickpeas, and Cheesy Cauliflower Pot Pie, to name just a few. Pasta lovers will be amazed by the entire chapter dedicated to a range of silky-smooth, creamy sauces with hidden veggies. Plus, you'll never believe that rich, decadent desserts like Sticky Date Pudding and Stone Fruit Cobbler are vegan, with no unusual ingredients needed.

Whether you're a longtime vegan or are just starting to prepare plant-forward dishes, *Cozy Vegan*—filled with one hundred flavorful recipes, time-saving tips, and cooking hacks—makes it easier than ever to live a more wholesome, plant-based life.

Cozy Vegan

100 Delicious, Plant-Based Comfort Food Recipes

Liz Douglas

SIMON ELEMENT

New York Amsterdam/Antwerp London
Toronto Sydney/Melbourne New Delhi

SIMON
ELEMENT

An Imprint of Simon & Schuster, LLC
1230 Avenue of the Americas
New York, NY 10020

Originally published in Australia in 2025 by Affirm Press

First Simon Element hardcover edition January 2026

Interior design by Andy Warren Design © Affirm Press

Manufactured in China

1 3 5 7 9 10 8 6 4 2

Library of Congress Control Number: 2025939106

ISBN 978-1-6682-0974-5
ISBN 978-1-6682-0975-2 (ebook)

For Mum and Dad

Con

tents

Welcome

Whether you are just dipping your toe into the world of plant-forward food or you're already vegan, this book is here to make cooking with plants as simple and delicious as possible.

You'll find many familiar comfort foods here, but made with a plant-based twist and packed with flavor. This collection of one hundred hearty and wholesome recipes will give you some new and exciting options for everyday meals, plus a few sweet treats, of course (because what is life without those?). I was lucky enough to have lots of independent recipe testers work with me, and you'll find their personal recommendations throughout the book.

I strive to make all my recipes accessible by using everyday ingredients as much as possible and avoiding expensive substitutes. That said, if you are new to vegan cooking, there may be a few pantry essentials worth picking up. You'll see these called for over and over again to re-create the flavors or properties of meat, eggs, or dairy. Get yourself some textured vegetable protein (TVP), nutritional yeast, flaxseed, tapioca flour, soy sauce, and miso paste, plus a good-quality blender, and you should be set. Oh, and always be sure to buy the right kind of tofu as specified in each recipe. Then go forth on your plant-based kitchen adventures!

From my home to yours,

Liz

Basics

If there was just one cheese substitute that I insist you try, it would have to be this one. It only takes 5 minutes and is loved by vegans and non-vegans alike. I used to describe it as a replacement for the dry parmesan cheese powder you find in the grocery aisle, but over the years I have found it to be far more versatile than that. So although I call it parmesan, you can think of this as more of a handy savory-booster. It is addictive.

This well-loved vegan staple is typically made with cashews. Most of the flavor comes from the nutritional yeast, though, so you can use any mild-tasting nut or seed you prefer. I have listed some of my favorite options in this recipe, and each has its own subtle flavor difference. Try sprinkling this on pasta, soups, salads, roast veggies or any savory dish.

Seed or Nut Parmesan

TOTAL TIME: 5 MINUTES
MAKES 1 LARGE JAR

1 cup seeds or nuts (cashews, blanched almonds, pumpkin seeds or sunflower seeds work well)
1 cup nutritional yeast
1 tsp salt

1. Place all the ingredients in a blender (I prefer a small bullet-style blender) and pulse for a few seconds, then give it a shake or stir to mix up the ingredients. Pulse again for another 1–2 seconds. It's important not to blend for too long or it will turn into a paste. A few small chunks of seeds or nuts are fine.
2. Store in an airtight jar in the pantry for up to three weeks.

This easy spice mixture is a huge *time saver if you want to make substitutes like Tofu Scramble (see page 38), Pumpkin Seed Scramble (see page 58), or Mini Quiches (see page 56). Combining all your spices in advance will save you the tedium of searching around every time you want to enjoy a high-protein eggy brekky.*

Eggy Spice Mix

TOTAL TIME: 10 MINUTES
SERVES 6

1 cup nutritional yeast
1 tbsp smoked paprika
2 tsp garlic powder
2 tsp onion powder or granulated onion
2 tsp ground turmeric
2 tsp kala namak (black salt)
½ tsp cracked pepper

1. Put all the ingredients in an airtight glass jar or container and shake thoroughly to mix. Store in the pantry or a cool, dry place for up to six months.
2. Refer to specific recipes for quantities of this spice mix, but as a rule of thumb, add 1 tablespoon of spice mix to every 3½ ounces (100g) of base ingredient (like tofu or pumpkin seeds).

In my pre-vegan days, I was a real cheese lover—whether it was the smelliest of blue cheeses, runny camembert, or your bog-standard tasty cheddar, I was up for it.

So naturally, cheese was one of the first foods I began to experiment with after going vegan. At one point I was so obsessed that I had multiple varieties in every corner of the kitchen: a dripping cheesecloth strung from the kitchen tap, an aging camembert sitting in the pantry or a feta marinating in the fridge. I even considered buying a dedicated wine fridge to maintain the perfect temperature for aging and mold development. I had so many on the go that my husband joked he would one day be greeted by a sentient cheese in the kitchen.

But after a while and some very mixed results, I decided to leave the specialty cheeses to the experts. I turned my focus to an easier everyday option instead: cheddar.

This recipe is the result: an affordable and mild vegan cheese that actually melts! You can store it in the freezer and grate some off as you need it.

Melty Cheddar Cheese

TOTAL TIME: 35 MINUTES
MAKES 1 LARGE BALL (ABOUT 1 POUND/500G)

½ cup raw cashews
2 cups unsweetened soy milk
½ cup tapioca flour
¼ cup nutritional yeast
2 tbsp apple cider vinegar
2½ tbsp white miso paste
1 tsp Dijon mustard

1. Place the cashews in a bowl and cover with some boiling water. Soak for 15 minutes, then drain and rinse in cold water.
2. Place the soaked cashews and all the remaining ingredients in a blender and blitz until smooth. Taste and add salt as desired.
3. Transfer the mixture to a saucepan and bring to a simmer over medium-low heat. Reduce heat to low and continue to stir for 1–2 minutes until the mixture becomes a thick, melted-cheese consistency. Remove from heat.
4. The cheese can be eaten immediately in this melted consistency. If saving it for later, shape the mixture into a rough ball and store in an airtight container in the freezer for up to two months. Shred the frozen cheese with a grater when ready to use. Add it to toasted sandwiches, pizza, tacos, mashed potatoes, or any other recipe where melted cheese would be used. Return any remaining cheese to the freezer promptly.

The perfect topping for Mexican-inspired meals, this nacho cheese sauce is made stretchy by using a little tapioca flour. Try it on Loaded Nachos (see page 84) or even on its own as a dip.

Nacho Cheese Sauce

TOTAL TIME: 15 MINUTES
SERVES 4

- 2 tbsp brine from a jar of jalapeños
- 1½ cups unsweetened soy milk
- ⅓ cup plant-based butter or olive oil
- 1 tbsp all-purpose flour
- 1 tbsp tapioca starch
- ½ cup nutritional yeast
- 2 tbsp white miso paste
- 1 tbsp garlic powder
- 2 tsp smoked paprika

1. In a glass measuring cup, stir together the brine and soy milk then set aside for 2–3 minutes to thicken.
2. Put the butter or olive oil in a small saucepan over medium-low heat. Once the butter has melted or the oil is hot, add the flour and stir for 2 minutes. Whisk in the tapioca starch, nutritional yeast, miso paste, garlic powder, and smoked paprika to combine, then gradually add the thickened soy milk mixture, whisking constantly to avoid lumps.
3. Increase the heat to medium-high and simmer for 2–3 minutes until the sauce becomes thick and a little stretchy. Serve immediately on nachos or with tacos.

NOTES

Want a plain stretchy cheese sauce without the nacho flavor? Omit the smoked paprika and replace the brine with more soy milk.

You can also substitute the soy milk with any unsweetened nut or oat milk, but keep in mind that its viscosity and flavor will impact the final dish. I typically use soy milk for cheese, as it is very creamy, or oat milk as an alternative. I would not recommend coconut or rice milk. Coconut milk (even the type for drinking) has a noticeable flavor, and rice milk tends to be too sweet for savory cooking.

The simple, readily available ingredients create such a lovely cheesy flavor with a zing. Love the addition of the jalapeño brine! I always use the same trick for my "feta" spread—it gives a nice hint of something something. And souring the soy milk before cooking was a surprise. Very easy instructions, no blender necessary, just a nice whisk. No lumps! – Kerstin

My husband is the quick pickle afficionado in our house. He whips up a batch every few weeks, so I now consider it a staple and have become accustomed to a certain pickly way of living. We always have a jar in the pantry and fridge.

This easy-peasy red onion and red cabbage mix comes together very quickly and can be used as a topping on any savory meal that needs a little sour oomph. I especially love it on tacos, curries, and sandwiches. Make a big batch now and thank yourself later.

Quickle

TOTAL TIME: 15 MINUTES + 30 MINUTES PICKLING TIME
MAKES ABOUT 4 × 2-CUP (16OZ/500ML) JARS

- 2 red onions, very thinly sliced (1⁄16 inch/1–2mm)
- 2 cups red cabbage, very thinly sliced (1⁄16 inch/1–2mm)
- 3 cups distilled white vinegar
- 3 cups water
- ½ cup sugar
- ½ tsp red pepper flakes (optional)
- 3 tbsp salt

1. Add the sliced onions and cabbage to a large bowl and toss with your hands to combine. Transfer the onion and cabbage mixture into sterilized glass jars and pack down firmly.
2. Combine the vinegar, water, sugar, red pepper flakes (if using), and salt in a large saucepan. Bring to a boil, stirring frequently. Once the sugar has dissolved, pour the vinegar mixture into each jar so that the cabbage and onion are covered. Seal with the lids and allow to cool at room temperature. Leave for a minimum of 30 minutes before eating.
3. The quickle will last for about two months in the pantry. Once opened, keep in the fridge for up to two weeks.

NOTES

Spice up your life (or don't!)

Although this recipe calls for red pepper flakes, it's not very spicy. It mostly tastes very sour, with a little crunch and warming heat. But if you are sensitive to heat, skip the red pepper. You can also get creative and add any combination of herbs or spices you would like. Peppercorns, coriander seeds, mustard, dill, rosemary, or thyme would all be strong candidates.

Sterilizing

There are a couple of ways to sterilize jars, but I find boiling is the easiest. Here's how I do it:

First, begin by washing your glass jars and metal lids in hot water with dish soap, then rinse thoroughly. Keep the lids off the jars for sterilizing.

Put the jars and lids in a large pot and cover with plenty of water so they are fully submerged. Bring to a boil over high heat, then reduce to a rolling boil for 5 minutes. Use tongs to carefully remove the jars and lids from the water. Transfer to a cooling rack to air-dry.

A simple vegan cheese sauce that is so creamy and easy. Delicious on vegetables like broccoli or on pasta, it takes just 15 minutes to make from start to finish. I recommend making a fresh batch every time, as it loses its smooth texture when reheated.

Simple Cheesy Sauce

TOTAL TIME: 15 MINUTES
SERVES 4

1 cup raw cashews
½ cup unsweetened soy milk
juice of ½ lemon
1 garlic clove
1 tbsp nutritional yeast
⅓ cup water
2 tsp white miso paste

1. Place the cashews in a bowl and cover with some boiling water. Soak for 15 minutes, then drain and rinse in cold water.
2. Place the soaked cashews and all the remaining ingredients in a blender and blitz until smooth. Taste and add salt as desired. Add extra water if you'd like a thinner consistency.
3. Serve over vegetables, pasta, or any savory dish you like.

NOTES

You can substitute the soy milk with any unsweetened nut or oat milk, but keep in mind that its viscosity and flavor will impact the final dish. I typically use soy milk for cheese, as it is very creamy, or oat milk as an alternative.

I would not recommend coconut or rice milk. Coconut milk (even the type for drinking) has a noticeable flavor, and rice milk tends to be too sweet for savory cooking.

This sauce is best enjoyed fresh for the smoothest consistency. You can still enjoy leftovers; however, the sauce will thicken when cooled then reheated. Add a splash of soy milk or water to loosen it to the desired consistency.

You'll be amazed how much this sour cream both looks and tastes like the dairy version. It's ultra-creamy, smooth, and has a light, whipped consistency. Delicious on baked potatoes, soups, pasta, nachos, or any dish that would normally include sour cream.

Sour Cream

TOTAL TIME: 20 MINUTES
MAKES ABOUT 1 CUP

½ cup cashews
½ cup neutral vegetable oil
½ cup natural, unsweetened plant-based yogurt
juice of 1 lemon (2–3 tbsp)
½ tsp salt

1. Place the cashews in a bowl and cover with boiling water. Soak for 15 minutes, then drain and rinse in cold water.
2. Place the soaked cashews and all the remaining ingredients in a blender and blitz until smooth. Taste and add extra salt as desired. Transfer to a clean jar or airtight container and refrigerate for 1 hour to firm up.
3. Use as a topping on baked potatoes, nachos, soups, or any savory dish that would call for sour cream. Keep refrigerated in an airtight container for up to two days.

This simple and affordable yogurt recipe requires just three ingredients: cashews, soy milk, and probiotic culture. You will need some gear to make this—at minimum, a quality blender and a thermometer. Ideally, you'll also have a yogurt maker. It's not essential, but it will greatly improve your chances of success, especially if you're new to fermenting. See the recipe notes for my tips and tricks.

You might be thinking, why bother making yogurt when you can buy it? Well, there are four great reasons: price, taste, availability, and nutritional benefit. Many supermarket-brand vegan yogurts are made from coconut, which is delicious but high in saturated fat and low in protein. Nutritionally speaking, it's not comparable to dairy yogurt, and I consider it to be more of an occasional food or dessert. In contrast, this soy yogurt is high in protein and low in fat.

I also like to make my own yogurt because it's cheap, delicious, and versatile. My recipe is thick and creamy but unsweetened, so you have the option to use it in savory dishes like curries, sauces, and soups.

Plus, once you get the hang of making your own yogurt, it requires very little hands-on time (about 10 minutes); it just feels like a no-brainer!

Three-Ingredient Greek Yogurt

TOTAL TIME: 6 HOURS
SERVES 6

½ cup raw cashews
4 cups (1L) unsweetened soy milk
¼ cup plant-based yogurt or 1 packet of powdered yogurt starter

1. If you're organized, cover the cashews with water and leave overnight in the fridge. Alternatively, you can boil the cashews for 10 minutes, then drain and rinse under cold water. (If your blender is not high-powered, I'd recommend soaking the cashews overnight or boiling them for 25 minutes to make them extra soft.)
2. Put the cashews and ½ cup of the soy milk in a blender and blitz for 1 minute or until combined and completely smooth, with no grittiness.
3. Combine the blended cashews, remaining soy milk, and yogurt or starter in a saucepan over low heat, stirring constantly until it reaches 86°F (30°C).
4. Transfer to clean glass jars or a yogurt maker container and cover with lids.
5. To ferment, the yogurt needs to be kept at a consistently warm temperature for 4–6 hours. This gets the bacteria active and gives the yogurt its tangy flavor. It's important not to let the yogurt get too hot, though, or the heat will kill the bacteria. Leave the jar in a warm place (see notes for suggestions) or set the yogurt maker for 4 hours.
6. Taste the yogurt after 4 hours. It should have a mild tang and a smooth, thick, and set texture. You can make it tangier by leaving for an extra 1–2 hours, but any longer may cause the yogurt to split.
7. Chill the yogurt in the fridge for a few hours (it will get even thicker).

NOTES

While you can make this recipe without a yogurt maker, I highly recommend one. I got mine secondhand for twenty dollars, and it's one of the best-value appliances I've ever bought. You can still make yogurt by using jars and finding a warm spot in your house, though be aware that an inconsistent temperature means your yogurt won't set, which is very disappointing.

Here are my best tips for yogurt success:

- **Consistent temperature.** For yogurt to ferment, it must be kept at a consistently warm temperature of around 108°F (42°C) for 4–6 hours to activate the bacteria that create the tangy flavor. But anything over 120°F (49°C) will kill the bacteria, and under 90°F (32°C) means it won't ferment.
- **Ways to create a warm environment.** If you happen to live in a warm climate between 90°F and 108°F (32°C and 42°C), then you can leave your yogurt out at room temperature. Make sure it's not in direct sunlight or it will get too hot. Alternatively, you can flash-heat your oven to 400°F (200°C) for a few minutes, then turn it off, place the yogurt in the oven, leave the light on, and close the door. Check the temperature of the oven every hour or so and, if needed, intermittently turn it on and off at its lowest temperature so it stays between 90°F and 108°F (32°C and 42°C). Or you can heat a small room—a bathroom, closet, or laundry room—to provide a stable and cozy environment for your yogurt.
- **Use a good blender, not a food processor.** Otherwise the cashews won't blend properly and your yogurt will have a gritty texture.
- **Use a high-protein milk.** You must use soy or another high-protein plant milk for this recipe, otherwise the yogurt will not set and you will be left with a curdled mess (speaking from experience here). Almond, oat, or rice milk will not work.

Smoky, filling, and just a little greasy (in a good way!), this hangover savior ticks all the bacon-craving boxes. Make it in the oven or air fryer for a crispier result, or pan-fry for a classic, less chewy bacon.

Tofu Bacon

TOTAL TIME: ABOUT 1 HOUR
SERVES 4

1 pound (450g) extra firm tofu
⅓ cup soy sauce
1 tbsp maple syrup
1 tbsp smoked paprika

1. First, press the tofu. Place the tofu between sheets of paper towel or wrap it in a clean, non-fluffy tea towel. Weigh it down with a cutting board and some heavy objects for 10–20 minutes (a cast-iron dish or pan works nicely).
2. Slice the tofu into thin strips ⅛–¼ inch (3–5mm) wide. The thinner the strips, the crispier the bacon, but be careful not to make them too thin or they will easily tear.
3. In a small bowl, combine the soy sauce, maple syrup, and smoked paprika to make the marinade.
4. Place tofu pieces in a single layer in a large baking dish, pour over the marinade, and soak for at least 10 minutes. The longer you leave it, the more flavor the tofu will absorb.
5. To cook in an air fryer, place the tofu strips in the fryer for 18 minutes at 400°F (200°C), shaking halfway through.
   To cook in the oven, place the tofu on a lined baking sheet and bake at 400°F (210°C) for 20–25 minutes, flipping the pieces halfway through. They are done when golden and slightly crispy.
   To pan-fry, heat about 2 tablespoons of vegetable oil in a skillet over medium-high heat. Fry the tofu strips for 2–3 minutes on each side until golden. Drain on paper towel before serving; the tofu will get crispier after cooling.

A simple, classic vegan staple that is an affordable, dry, and crumbly substitute for Greek cheese. It won't melt, but it does have a very similar sharp and savory flavor. This is great in salads, quiches, and sandwiches.

Tofu Feta

TOTAL TIME: ABOUT 1 HOUR + 8 HOURS MARINATING TIME
MAKES 1 LARGE JAR

12 ounces (350g) extra firm tofu
¾ cup extra-virgin olive oil
juice of ½ medium lemon
3 tbsp apple cider vinegar
2 tsp salt
2 tsp whole peppercorns
¼ tsp red pepper flakes
1 garlic clove, minced
2 small sprigs rosemary
3 sprigs thyme

1. Press the tofu by placing the block between sheets of paper towel or wrapping in a clean, non-fluffy tea towel, then weighing it down with a cutting board and some heavy objects for a minimum of 30 minutes or up to 1 hour (a cast-iron dish or some heavy cookbooks work nicely).
2. In a medium mixing bowl, crumble the pressed tofu with your hands into rough ¾-inch (2cm) chunks. Some bigger bits are okay; just don't make it too fine.
3. In a separate large mixing bowl, whisk together the olive oil, lemon juice, apple cider vinegar, salt, peppercorns, red pepper flakes, and garlic to form the marinade. Add the tofu, rosemary, and thyme and mix to coat.
4. Transfer to a jar and seal. Leave in the fridge to marinate overnight before eating. It will keep refrigerated for about a week.

NOTES

There are a couple of things I'd like you to keep in mind when cooking with tofu. Firstly, it's critical to use the right kind of tofu—in this case, extra firm tofu, sometimes called hard tofu (classic or firm tofu ain't it). Anything other than extra firm or hard will be too soft and watery and simply will not work. It's also very important to press the tofu first to draw out as much water as possible. Think of it like a dense sponge that you are wringing out. We are going to use that sponge to mop up all the delicious flavors from the marinade. Yum!

If you can't get plant-based sweetened condensed milk easily, I have good news: it's very simple to make with just two ingredients, milk and sugar. You can use soy, oat, almond, or any other plant-based milk, but be careful not to overcook; it should still look quite thin when removed from the heat, but it will firm up as it cools. I have accidentally made vegan caramel sauce a few times by overcooking the mixture, so learn from my mistakes and always set a timer.

Two-Ingredient Sweetened Condensed Milk

TOTAL TIME: 40 MINUTES
MAKES 1 JAR

3 cups plant-based milk
1 cup sugar

1. Whisk the milk and sugar together in a large saucepan over medium-low heat. (It's important to use a large saucepan, as some milks will froth a lot and can easily overflow.) Keep whisking as you bring it to a low simmer. Continue to simmer for about 25–30 minutes or until the milk has reduced by half and the color has caramelized slightly, whisking gently now and then as it cooks so it doesn't burn. The final consistency should be thick and sticky but still pourable.
2. Store in a glass jar in the refrigerator for up to a week.

This easy and affordable replacement for sweet whipped cream is made using a can of chilled full-fat coconut cream. I first came across this beloved vegan hack when I was in my early twenties, a few years before I went plant-based, after volunteering to make a birthday cake for a friend who was allergic to dairy. I lathered the big vanilla slab cake in this whipped coconut cream and piled it with strawberries, and the coconut flavor and ultra-creamy mouthfeel blew me away. I actually preferred it to dairy, and it became my go-to whipped cream option. It's delicious with anything that is complementary to a coconut flavor. I particularly love it on a lemon cake or with scones and jam.

Now, although this is a very simple recipe, it can easily go wrong! There are two key tips to keep in mind.

Firstly, buy full-fat coconut cream with none of the crap: check the ingredients label and avoid anything that contains gums or emulsifiers. Coconut cream naturally separates from the water, but many brands now add emulsifiers or gums to prevent this. For our purposes, we want the coconut cream to separate from the water so we can get a nice, firm whip. If you try to whip one with emulsifiers, it will still taste good, but it will be runny.

Secondly, the unopened can needs to be chilled for at least 10 hours for the cream to separate, so remember to put it in the fridge the day before. I often keep a can in the back of the fridge in case I have a sudden urge for dessert (it happens). Also, keep in mind that coconut cream isn't as stable as whipped dairy cream. It will hold its shape served chilled or at room temperature, but will soften quickly on hot desserts or drinks.

Whipped Coconut Cream

TOTAL TIME: 11 HOURS
SERVES 6

2 (13.5-ounce/400ml) cans full-fat coconut cream
⅔ cup powdered sugar
2 tbsp cornstarch
tiny pinch of salt

1. Chill the unopened cans of coconut cream in the refrigerator overnight, or for at least 10 hours. Before whipping, chill your mixing bowl in the freezer for 15 minutes.
2. The coconut cream solids should have risen to the top of the cans and be very firm, and the coconut water should rest at the bottom. Scoop out the solids into the chilled mixing bowl and discard the water (or freeze it in an ice-cube tray for smoothies).
3. Add the powdered sugar and cornstarch to the solids and beat with an electric whisk or beaters until it begins to form peaks, about 1–2 minutes. Note that coconut cream won't be quite as stiff as regular dairy cream, and unlike dairy cream, it doesn't take long to whip. Be careful not to overwhip, as it will soften.
4. For an even firmer whip, chill the whipped cream in the refrigerator for 15–30 minutes before serving, checking the consistency occasionally. Don't leave it for too long or make it in advance, as it will eventually set hard again.

Break

fast

Tofu scramble is a plant-based staple. If you've never tried it, this is the go-to vegan replacement for scrambled eggs. This recipe allows you to customize it with your tofu of choice. Opt for silken tofu if you prefer a light, pillowy consistency. Extra firm is crumbly and dense. Use firm tofu if you'd like it somewhere in the middle. I usually go for extra firm tofu, as it has the highest protein content, but this is delicious any way. Try each of them and see which you prefer.

If you are making tofu scramble regularly, it's worth making a big batch of my Eggy Spice Mix (see page 14)—it will save you so much time! You will need 4 tablespoons of it in this recipe if you make the big batch, but if not, I've also listed out the exact amount of the spices you will need for this recipe as a one-off.

Tofu Scramble

TOTAL TIME: 15 MINUTES
SERVES 2

12 ounces (350g) tofu (silken, firm or extra firm)
1 tbsp Dijon mustard
1 tbsp olive oil
¼–⅓ cup unsweetened plant-based milk
buttered toast or English muffin to serve

EGGY SPICE MIX
2 tbsp nutritional yeast
½ tsp smoked paprika
½ tsp garlic powder
½ tsp onion powder or granulated onion
½ tsp ground turmeric
¼ tsp kala namak (black salt)
¼ tsp cracked black pepper

1. Put the tofu in a large mixing bowl. If using firm or extra firm tofu, crumble it with your hands. Add the spice mix and Dijon mustard to the tofu and stir to combine. If using silken tofu, it should break apart as you do this.
2. Place a skillet over medium heat and add the olive oil. Once hot, add the tofu mixture to the pan.
3. Start with ¼ cup of the milk and pour it over the tofu then stir. If you want a creamier and softer scramble, add more milk, up to ⅓ cup in total. You can add more milk during cooking if needed. If you find you have added too much, simmer to reduce.
4. Continue stirring until the scramble turns golden, usually about 5 minutes.
5. Serve on toast or an English muffin with sides of your choice.

NOTES

For the tofu newbies

Tofu comes in a range of textures, but the main ones are silken, firm and extra firm.

Silken tofu has the mildest flavor and a soft, delicate texture. It is often used as a dairy or egg replacement and is a popular choice for dessert recipes. It has a similar consistency to panna cotta or a gel-like set yogurt.

Firm tofu has a slightly bouncier, more resilient texture. It is lovely cubed in a broth-based soup. I use this tofu the least, as I find it less versatile than silken or extra firm.

Extra firm tofu is dense like a sponge. It has the lowest water content and the highest protein. It is firm enough that you can press it without breaking it. Pressing draws out extra water (like wringing a sponge) and primes the tofu to soak up marinades. Extra firm tofu is often used as a meat replacement.

Fast, one bowl, and no unusual ingredients! This simple banana bread is fragrant, moist and not too sweet. A humble baking classic that is delicious for breakfast, plain or toasted. You'd never know it's vegan.

Easy Banana Bread

TOTAL TIME: 55 MINUTES
MAKES 12 SLICES

3 medium overripe bananas, peeled, plus 1 extra for decoration (optional)
⅓ cup vegetable oil
⅓ cup brown sugar
½ tsp vanilla bean paste (or vanilla extract)
2 tbsp unsweetened plant-based milk
¼ tsp salt
1¾ cups all-purpose flour
2 tsp baking powder
2 tsp cinnamon

OPTIONAL EXTRAS (PICK ONE)

¼ cup walnuts, roughly chopped
¼ cup raisins
½ cup plant-based dark chocolate chips

1. Preheat the oven to 350°F (180°C). Lightly grease and line a 8½ × 4½-inch (21 × 11cm) loaf pan with parchment paper.
2. In a large bowl, mash three of the bananas until they form a smooth paste. Add the vegetable oil, brown sugar, vanilla, milk and salt. Mix well to combine.
3. Sift the flour, baking powder and cinnamon over the wet mixture and add any optional extras (if using). Mix until just combined then scrape the batter into the loaf pan.
4. If using, slice the extra banana in half lengthways and gently press it into the top of the batter.
5. Bake for 45–50 minutes or until a skewer inserted into the center comes out clean.
6. Leave to cool in the pan for 5 minutes, then lift out to a wire rack to cool completely. Cut into slices and serve.

NOTES

The extra banana on the top looks super cute, but it is completely optional and just as delicious without. I leave it off unless I am baking the banana bread for somebody else or for special occasions, like cookbook photo shoots!

Banana bread tastes extra indulgent toasted and topped with a generous smear of almond butter. Is it the lightest breakfast option? No, but trust me and do it anyway.

Not as cloyingly sweet as some recipes I've tried . . . This is truly a bread, not a cake. Lovely! – Kerstin

Easy and [ingredients] in the pantry—best kinda recipe! And not needing any special vegan butter or egg substitute. It was really hard to wait for it to cool before cutting it! Smelled amazing. – Mandi

If you're not big on breakfast, prepping something that tastes like dessert is always a good choice. These bars look decadent but are very wholesome and made with oats, flaxseed, banana, and nuts. Prep them in advance and enjoy throughout the week as a healthy treat or light and tasty breakfast.

Breakfast Berry Chia Bars

TOTAL TIME: 40 MINUTES
MAKES 12

2 tbsp ground flaxseed
6 tbsp water
1 medium overripe banana, mashed
2 tbsp maple syrup
¼ cup unsweetened plant-based milk
1 tsp vanilla extract
1½ cups rolled oats
1 tsp baking powder
1 tsp cinnamon
⅛ tsp salt
2½ cups frozen berries (strawberries, raspberries, blueberries or a mix)
2 tbsp chia seeds

CRUMBLE TOPPING
⅓ cup quick oats
¼ cup almond meal
¼ cup walnuts or pecans, finely chopped
2 tbsp coconut oil, melted
3 tbsp maple syrup
½ tsp cinnamon

1. Preheat the oven to 350°F (180°C) and line a 8 × 8-inch (20 × 20cm) square baking dish with parchment paper.
2. In a small bowl, combine the ground flaxseed with the water. Leave for 5 minutes until it becomes thick and gelatinous.
3. In a large mixing bowl, mash the banana. Add the flaxseed mixture, maple syrup, milk and vanilla extract and mix to combine. Add the rolled oats, baking powder, cinnamon and salt and mix again until combined.
4. Transfer the mixture to the lined baking dish and press down with the back of a spoon to flatten. Bake in the oven for 15 minutes.
5. Put the berries in a small pot and simmer over medium heat for 3–4 minutes or until they start to release their juices. Turn off the heat and stir through the chia seeds.
6. Wipe out the first mixing bowl and add all crumble topping ingredients, mixing to combine. It will have a dry and coarse texture.
7. Remove the base from the oven and top with the berry mixture then the crumble topping. Bake for 10 minutes or until crumble is a light golden brown.
8. Leave to cool in the pan for 15 minutes before slicing into twelve bars. Store in an airtight container in the refrigerator for up to five days.

This chia mousse tastes like dessert but is actually healthy. It's not overly sweet but it is very chocolatey, thanks to the cacao powder. It's also a source of omega-3s and fiber, which will help keep you full throughout the morning. It takes minutes to throw together and is a great recipe to make in advance for the workweek ahead. I love it as a healthy treat to look forward to with my morning coffee.

Choc Chia Mousse

TOTAL TIME: 10 MINUTES + 3 HOURS CHILLING TIME
MAKES 4

2 cups unsweetened plant-based milk
½ cup chia seeds
¼ cup cacao powder
¼ cup maple syrup
1 tsp vanilla extract or paste

TO SERVE (OPTIONAL)
plant-based yogurt
fresh raspberries

1. Blitz all the ingredients on high in a blender until smooth (2–3 minutes). Transfer to four individual jars or airtight containers. Seal the jars or containers, then chill in the fridge overnight (or for at least 3 hours).
2. Enjoy as is or top it with yogurt and raspberries to make it extra tasty.

NOTES

Though very similar to cocoa powder, cacao powder is generally processed at lower temperatures, preserving more flavor and antioxidants. Find it in the health food aisle of most supermarkets or buy it online.

In a pinch, cocoa powder will also work fine. The mousse may taste sweeter and less chocolatey.

I love a healthy breakfast disguised as dessert. Inspired by a chocolate banoffee pie, this layered breakfast cup tastes as good as it looks. It's made with a base of rolled oats and walnuts, then topped with Choc Chia Mousse (see page 46), banana, and yogurt. Easy to prep, it's full of fiber, omega-3s and protein to keep you full and energized all morning.

Choc Banoffee Breakfast Cup

TOTAL TIME: 10 MINUTES + 3 HOURS CHILLING TIME
MAKES 4

CRUMBLE BASE
¾ cup rolled oats
¼ cup crushed walnuts or pecans
2 tbsp coconut oil, melted
1 tbsp coconut sugar

CHOCOLATE FILLING
2 cups unsweetened plant-based milk
½ cup chia seeds
¼ cup cacao powder
¼ cup maple syrup
1 tsp vanilla extract or paste

TOPPINGS
2 medium bananas, peeled and sliced
2 cups plant-based yogurt

1. For the crumble base, blitz all the ingredients on high in a blender until they reach a coarse, sandy texture. Divide between four jars or glasses. Wipe out the blender.
2. For the chocolate filling, blitz all the ingredients on high in a blender until smooth (2–3 minutes). Divide the mousse between the jars, layering on top of the crumble base. Cover the jars and chill in the fridge overnight (or for at least 3 hours). These will keep in the fridge for up to five days.
3. When you're ready to eat, top each with sliced banana and yogurt.

These corn fritters are an easy but delicious brunch option. Don't skip the zingy Avocado Crema (see page 194) for a fresh finish.

These are crispiest if made with fresh corn, but you can also use frozen or canned. The latter contain more water, so you may need to add a little extra cornstarch to compensate.

Corn Fritters with Zingy Avocado Crema

TOTAL TIME: 40 MINUTES
MAKES 12

2 tbsp ground flaxseed
6 tbsp water
4 ears of corn or around 3 cups corn kernels
½ cup loosely packed cilantro leaves
¼ cup unsweetened plant-based milk
½ red onion, finely diced
½ cup whole wheat flour
½ tsp baking powder
¼ cup cornstarch
½ tsp smoked paprika
½ tsp ground cumin
½ tsp salt
3 tbsp vegetable oil

TO SERVE
Avocado Crema (page 194)
extra cilantro leaves
lime wedges

1. Set your oven to its lowest temperature (around 150°F/70°C is fine).
2. Prepare flax eggs by combining the ground flaxseed with the water in a large mixing bowl. Set aside for 5 minutes until thick and gelatinous.
3. Slice the kernels from the ears of corn; you'll need about 3 cups. Finely chop the cilantro leaves.
4. Add the milk to the flax eggs and stir to combine. Add the remaining fritter ingredients except the oil and mix well. There should be just enough batter to bind the corn, onion and cilantro together.
5. Place a large skillet over medium-high heat and add half the oil. Once hot, scoop up roughly ¼ cup portions of batter with wet hands and gently shape into patties. Try to make them as thin as possible without falling apart.
6. Fry for 3–4 minutes, then flip and fry for another 3 minutes until golden and cooked through. Place the cooked fritters on a wire rack in the oven to keep warm. Add the last of the oil to the pan if needed and cook the remaining batter.
7. Serve topped with Avocado Crema and extra cilantro leaves with lime wedges.

Convenient, delicious, and high in protein, these freezer burritos are the perfect grab-and-go breakfast. My version uses textured vegetable protein instead of sausage and tofu scramble for egg. If you reheat these naked in an air fryer or oven, the tortilla will become super crispy, like a pie. YUM. Enjoy with a drizzle of hot sauce, and if you want to make it a more dignified meal, pile up a big salad on the side.

Freezer Breakfast Burritos

TOTAL TIME: 40 MINUTES
MAKES 6

2 tbsp vegetable oil
6 large tortillas
3 tbsp plant-based mayonnaise, store bought or homemade (page 208)

TVP FILLING
1 cup textured vegetable protein
1 tsp vegetable bouillon powder
1 cup boiling water
2 tbsp nutritional yeast
2 tbsp soy sauce
1 tbsp maple syrup
1 tsp ground fennel seeds
½ tsp ground sage
½ tsp ground black pepper
¼ tsp ground coriander
¼ tsp smoked paprika
¼ tsp garlic powder
¼ tsp onion powder

PEPPER TOFU SCRAMBLE
12 ounces (350g) extra firm tofu
2 tbsp nutritional yeast
½ tsp smoked paprika
½ tsp garlic powder
½ tsp onion powder
½ tsp ground turmeric
¼ tsp kala namak (black salt)
¼ tsp cracked black pepper

1. To make the filling, rehydrate the textured vegetable protein (TVP) in a medium mixing bowl with the bouillon powder and boiling water. Set aside for 5 minutes. Once the TVP has absorbed most of the liquid, add the remaining filling ingredients and mix well to combine.
2. Heat the vegetable oil in a medium skillet over medium heat. Add the TVP mixture to the pan and cook for 5–7 minutes, stirring frequently. Season with salt to taste, then remove from heat.
3. To make the pepper tofu scramble, crumble the tofu into a large mixing bowl with your hands. Add the nutritional yeast, smoked paprika, garlic powder, onion powder, turmeric, kala namak, black pepper, Dijon mustard and milk. Stir to combine. Put the olive oil in a large skillet over medium heat and fry the onion and red and green peppers for 1 minute, stirring. Add the garlic and continue stirring for 1 minute before adding the tofu mixture. Continue to stir for 7–10 minutes until the tofu scramble is bright yellow and has some golden highlights. Remove from the heat.
4. To assemble, place a tortilla-sized sheet of parchment paper on top of a sheet of aluminum foil. Lay a tortilla on the parchment paper then spread half a tablespoon of mayonnaise over the center of each tortilla. Spoon some TVP filling and tofu scramble in a line down the center, leaving about an inch (a few centimeters) margin at the ends.
5. Fold the burrito by tucking the two short sides inward over the filling, then rolling the long sides over the filling, tucking firmly as you go. Eat immediately or store by wrapping tightly in the parchment paper and aluminum foil, twisting the ends to seal. Store in the refrigerator for up to three days or in the freezer for up to two months.

- 1 tbsp Dijon mustard
- ⅓ cup unsweetened plant-based milk
- 1 tbsp olive oil
- ½ red onion, finely diced
- ½ red bell pepper, finely diced
- ½ green bell pepper, finely diced
- 2 garlic cloves, crushed

REHEATING FROM FROZEN

Microwave: Remove the aluminum foil layer and microwave wrapped in parchment paper on high for 2–3 minutes until heated right through the center.

Air fryer: Remove aluminum foil layer and microwave on high for 90 seconds or until thawed. If you'd like the burrito to be crispy, unwrap and place the naked burrito seam side down on the air fryer basket. If you prefer a softer tortilla, leave it fully wrapped. Air fry at 400°F (200°C) for 4 minutes, then flip sides and air fry for another 3 minutes until golden and crispy.

Oven: Preheat the oven to 350°F (180°C). If you'd like the burrito to be crispy, unwrap the foil and parchment paper and place on a lined baking sheet, seam side down. If you prefer a softer tortilla, leave it fully wrapped. Bake from frozen for 30–40 minutes, flipping halfway through.

Full of flavor and very quick to cook on the stove. – Briana

This healthier twist on banana bread is a delicious way to get extra vegetables into your day. It's a fun, vibrant green snack with almost no spinach flavor but with extra fiber and antioxidants. It is great for kids, and if preferred, you can omit the sugar and it will still have a slightly sweet flavor from the bananas.

Green Banana Bread

TOTAL TIME: 1 HOUR
MAKES 12 SLICES

1 cup all-purpose flour
1 cup whole wheat flour
2 tsp baking powder
¼ tsp salt
¼ cup sugar (optional)
3 medium overripe bananas, peeled
½ cup unsweetened plant-based milk
¼ cup mild vegetable oil or melted coconut oil
2 cups (55g) loosely packed baby spinach
1 tsp vanilla extract

1. Preheat the oven to 350°F (180°C). Line a 8½ × 4½-inch (21 × 11cm) (base measurement) loaf pan with parchment paper.
2. In a large mixing bowl, sift the flours and baking powder together. Add the salt and sugar (if using) and stir to combine.
3. Put the bananas, milk, vegetable oil, spinach leaves and vanilla extract in a blender and blitz on high until smooth, about 1–2 minutes. Pour into the dry mixture and stir until just combined.
4. Pour the batter into the prepared loaf pan and bake for 50 minutes. Insert a skewer in the center to check if it's done—if it comes out clean, it should be ready. If it comes out with batter stuck to it, return to the oven for another 5 minutes and test again. Once ready, remove from the oven and leave to cool for 10 minutes before transferring to a cooling rack for another 10 minutes.
5. Slice and enjoy.

NOTES

This batter can also be used to make muffins, which make a great handheld snack for littles. Reduce the baking time to 20 minutes, then check if done with the skewer test and bake for an additional 5 minutes if needed.

TIP

Overripe bananas make all the difference when it comes to making sweet, fragrant banana bread. They are especially important in this recipe if you choose to omit the sugar, as they help mask any hint of spinach flavor. I love a bargain so I'll usually try to buy my bananas discounted at my local shop. If you need to ripen bananas quickly, try popping them into a paper bag (with an avocado if you have one) and they should ripen up nicely within a day.

Mini quiches are a quintessential Aussie snack. They remind me of picnics with high school friends at our town's local Melbourne Cup day. (My childhood and teenage years were not very vegan.)

Tofu skeptics, please set your doubts aside—these taste like the real deal, I promise. Plus, they are convenient, protein-rich and freeze well.

Consider the toppings in the recipe below a suggestion and use whatever you like. Classic combinations include tomato and tofu bacon, spinach and mushroom, or roast pumpkin or squash and feta. These are also perfect for lunch boxes—my son, Oliver, is a big fan.

Mini Quiches

TOTAL TIME: 1 HOUR
MAKES 6

1 pound (450g) extra firm tofu
5 tbsp unsweetened plant-based milk
4 tbsp Eggy Spice Mix (page 14)
2 sheets plant-based puff pastry, thawed
¼ cup semi-dried or plump oil-packed sun-dried tomatoes, chopped
¼ cup kalamata olives, pitted

1. Preheat the oven to 350°F (180°C). Lightly grease a large six-hole muffin pan.
2. Break the tofu into pieces and add to a blender along with the milk and Eggy Spice Mix. Blitz for 1 minute or until smooth, stopping to scrape down the sides if needed.
3. Cut the pastry sheets into quarters and press 6 of them into the muffin pan (save or discard the others). Pour the tofu filling into each pastry shell and add some tomatoes and olives to each. Press the toppings into the filling so they are partly submerged.
4. Bake for 45 minutes, then leave in the pan for 10–15 minutes before serving to let the tofu firm up a little. These also taste great cold and will keep in the fridge for three days.

Believe it or not, pumpkin seeds can be transformed into a tasty, high-protein breakfast scramble. It doesn't taste like eggs exactly, but it is delicious and filling. It's also straightforward to make: combine soaked pumpkin seeds with spices and milk in a blender, then pan-fry.

Pumpkin Seed Scramble

TOTAL TIME: 20 MINUTES
SERVES 2

1 cup (130g) pumpkin seeds (pepitas)
½ cup unsweetened plant-based milk
2 tbsp Eggy Spice Mix (page 14)
1 tbsp olive oil
buttered toast or English muffin to serve

1. Place the pumpkin seeds in a small bowl and cover with boiling water. Soak for 10 minutes to soften, then drain and rinse under cold water.
2. Add the drained pumpkin seeds, milk and Eggy Spice Mix to a blender and blitz until smooth. Taste and season with extra salt if desired.
3. Heat the olive oil in a medium skillet. Reduce heat to medium, then add the pumpkin seed mixture. Cook for around 5 minutes, stirring constantly. The mixture will thicken as you heat it; add a splash of extra milk to make a thinner consistency if desired.
4. Serve immediately on toast or an English muffin.

Sometimes the best meals are the simplest ones. This is a layer of smooth tofu ricotta roasted with cherry tomatoes until blistering and sweet. I love this as an easy weekend brunch option (great if you're hosting), as you can make the tofu ricotta ahead of time.

If you are looking to spruce up any leftovers, you can also remove the tomatoes from the vine and blend this into a smooth and creamy pasta sauce.

Roasted Tomatoes with Tofu Ricotta

TOTAL TIME: 40 MINUTES
SERVES 4

1½ pounds (700g) cherry, grape or small tomatoes on the vine, or a mix
1 tbsp olive oil
¼ tsp salt
pinch of cracked black pepper
sourdough toast to serve

TOFU RICOTTA
1 pound (450g) extra firm tofu
½ cup almond meal
1 tbsp hemp seeds
juice of 1 lemon
2 tbsp olive oil
2 garlic cloves
2 tsp dried basil
1½ tsp salt
¼ cup nutritional yeast
pinch of ground black pepper

1. Preheat the oven to 375°F (190°C).
2. For the tofu ricotta, crumble the tofu into a food processor. Add the remaining ingredients and blend on high for 1 minute or until well combined. Stop occasionally to scrape down the sides if needed. The finished result should be a thick, creamy, ricotta-like consistency. Some small lumps are fine.
3. Put the tomatoes in a bowl, drizzle with the olive oil, sprinkle with the salt and pepper and toss with your hands to coat. Spread the tofu ricotta across the base of a roughly 10 × 7-inch (26 × 18cm) baking dish, then place the tomatoes on top. Roast for 25–30 minutes or until the tomatoes burst and blister.
4. Serve with toasted sourdough bread. Be careful not to burn your mouth, as the tomato juices will be very hot.

When I moved to Melbourne for university, I immediately became a brunch girl. Baked eggs were one of the first trendy options I discovered. The rich baked tomato sauce was so satisfying, and I also loved how the eggs looked like little prizes nestled in it. When I made this recipe, I wasn't sure whether to include an egg substitute, as they can be tricky, but I also wanted to create a vegan version with that visual wow factor. So I added tofu, and while it doesn't have the same texture as eggs, it looks and tastes fantastic. Plus tofu adds protein, and there is a hint of eggy flavor from the spices.

This shakshuka is easily my favorite breakfast. Make it for brunch on the weekend—it's excellent mopped up with some crusty sourdough.

Shakshuka

TOTAL TIME: 1 HOUR 10 MINUTES
SERVES 4

TOFU
11 ounces (300g) extra firm tofu
2 tbsp soy sauce
4 tbsp cornstarch
½ tsp kala namak (black salt)
¼ tsp cracked pepper
4 tbsp vegetable oil

SHAKSHUKA
1 tbsp olive oil
1 onion, finely diced
3 garlic cloves, crushed
½ red bell pepper, finely diced
1 (14-ounce/400g) can chickpeas, drained and rinsed
2 tbsp tomato paste
1 tsp sugar
2 tsp smoked paprika
2 tsp ground cumin
½ tsp ground coriander
½ tsp sumac
¼ tsp dried chili powder
¼ tsp cinnamon
½ tsp salt
⅓ cup stuffed or pitted green olives
⅓ cup semi-dried or plump oil-packed sun-dried tomatoes, roughly chopped
1 (28-ounce/800g) can diced tomatoes
¾ cup water

YOGURT SAUCE
2 tbsp lemon juice
2 tsp tahini
¼ cup natural, unsweetened plant-based yogurt

TO SERVE
sliced avocado
fresh cilantro leaves
toasted sourdough bread

1. Press the tofu by placing the block between sheets of paper towel or wrapping in a clean, non-fluffy tea towel and weighing it down with a cutting board and some heavy objects for a minimum of 30 minutes or up to 1 hour (a cast-iron dish or heavy cookbooks work nicely).
2. Break the pressed tofu into eight rough chunks and place in a large mixing bowl. Coat in the soy sauce and leave for 2 minutes to soak, then coat in the cornstarch, kala namak and pepper. Heat the vegetable oil in a medium ovenproof skillet over high heat. There should be about ⅜ inch (1cm) of vegetable oil in the bottom of the pan; add more if needed. Once the oil is hot, fry the tofu on all sides until golden and crispy. Remove to a plate lined with paper towel to absorb excess oil.
3. To make the shakshuka, reduce the heat in your pan to medium and add the olive oil. Fry the onion for 2–3 minutes until translucent. Add the garlic, bell pepper and chickpeas and continue stirring for another 3 minutes. Add the tomato paste, sugar, spices, salt, olives and semi-dried tomatoes and stir well for 1–2 minutes until coated, then add the diced tomatoes and water and simmer for 10 minutes. Nestle the tofu chunks into the sauce, then bake in the oven for 20 minutes.
4. For the yogurt sauce, whisk the lemon juice and tahini together until smooth, then mix in the yogurt and a pinch of salt.
5. Garnish the shakshuka in the baking dish with dollops of yogurt sauce, sliced avocado and fresh cilantro leaves and let everybody help themselves, with some sourdough toast on the side.

This easy breakfast pudding is perfect for hot summer days when you crave something cool and refreshing the minute you wake up. The flavors of banana, mango and passionfruit make you feel like you're on holiday every day.

Tropical Chia Pudding

TOTAL TIME: 10 MINUTES + 3 HOURS CHILLING TIME
SERVES 6

1 cup mashed overripe banana (about 2 bananas)
2 cups unsweetened plant-based milk
½ cup chia seeds
½ tsp vanilla extract
2 mangoes, peeled and diced (or substitute 1¾ cups/300g frozen mango, thawed)
2 passionfruit (or substitute ¼ cup frozen passionfruit pulp, thawed)
toasted coconut flakes to serve (optional)

1. Combine the mashed banana, milk, chia seeds and vanilla extract in a large bowl. Mix well to combine. Cover and chill in the refrigerator for 30 minutes, then mix again to ensure it is well combined.
2. If using thawed frozen mango, blitz in a blender until a smooth, thick puree.
3. Divide half the mango between six jars or containers. Top with roughly half the chia mixture. Repeat with the remaining mango and chia mixture to form two layers of each.
4. Halve the passionfruit and scoop out the pulp. Add some to the top of each chia pudding, then chill for at least 3 hours, or up to three days. When you're ready to eat, sprinkle on some toasted coconut flakes if using and enjoy!

Quick, easy, pretty to look at, healthful, versatile—great for snacks, breakfast or dessert. I will use the basic recipe and vary the fruit based on time of year and what's available. – Kate

So easy and fun. Great for meal prep and very low-effort cooking. – Erin

This hearty, veggie-packed savory breakfast will fuel a busy day. Mildly spiced (but not spicy), it is made with potatoes as the base plus tempeh and black beans for protein.

Breakfast Hash

TOTAL TIME: 45 MINUTES
SERVES 4

4 tbsp olive oil
3 large potatoes, peeled and cut into ¾-inch (2cm) cubes
½ tsp salt
¼ tsp cracked pepper
1 onion, diced
11 ounces (300g) tempeh, crumbled
½ red bell pepper, cut into ¾-inch (2cm) pieces
½ green bell pepper, cut into ¾-inch (2cm) pieces
3 garlic cloves, crushed
1 tbsp soy sauce
2 tsp smoked paprika
2 tsp ground cumin
1 tsp ground coriander
½ tsp ground turmeric
1 (14-ounce/400g) can black beans, drained and rinsed
2 cups loosely packed baby spinach

TO SERVE
sliced avocado
halved cherry tomatoes
cilantro leaves
lime wedges

1. Add 3 tablespoons of the olive oil to a large skillet over medium heat. Once hot, fry the potatoes with the salt and pepper for 3 minutes, stirring frequently. Reduce heat to low, cover with a lid and cook for 15–20 minutes or until the potatoes are tender, removing the lid and gently stirring every couple of minutes to avoid burning. Once the potatoes are tender and golden on all sides, remove from heat.
2. In a separate medium-sized skillet, heat the remaining tablespoon of olive oil and sauté the onion for 2–3 minutes until translucent. Add the crumbled tempeh and bell peppers and cook for an additional 3 minutes. Add the garlic, soy sauce, paprika, ground cumin, ground coriander and turmeric. Stir well for 2 minutes or until fragrant.
3. Add the black beans to the tempeh mixture and continue to cook for 3 minutes, stirring frequently. Add the baby spinach and stir until it wilts, about 2–3 minutes. Add the potatoes and gently stir to combine. Taste and season with more salt and pepper if desired.
4. Serve garnished with the avocado, tomatoes, cilantro leaves and a wedge of lime.

NOTES

Tempeh can be an acquired taste. I love it, but I am also quite particular and only buy one brand that I have grown accustomed to. If you're not a fan of tempeh, swap it for tofu, plant-based ground meat or rehydrated textured vegetable protein.

Easy, simple, yum. Super satisfying. Not complicated. Relatively quick. Packed with flavor and health. High enough in protein. Can be batch prepped. Will definitely be making this again. – Rachel

Love that it is packed with protein and vegetables. Nice hearty breakfast. – Christine

Soups,

Start

Sides,

and

ers

The epitome of simple, fresh food, this is the perfect no-fuss yet elegant side dish. This recipe is just two servings, so be sure to scale it up if you are hosting a group. It would pair well with Mushroom Galette (see page 128), Spanakopita (see page 140), Cheesy Cauliflower Pot Pie (see page 114), or Cauliflower and Cannellini Bean Gratin (see page 112).

Broccolini with Lemon Tahini Sauce and Toasted Almonds

TOTAL TIME: 15 MINUTES
SERVES 2

¼ cup almonds, roughly chopped
2 tsp olive oil
1 bunch broccolini, ends trimmed
1 tbsp water
¼ tsp salt
⅛ tsp freshly cracked black pepper
lemon wedges to serve

LEMON TAHINI SAUCE
¼ cup natural, unsweetened plant-based yogurt
2 tbsp tahini
juice of ¼ lemon
¼ tsp salt

1. Prepare the lemon tahini sauce by whisking all the ingredients together in a small bowl until it has a lightly whipped and creamy consistency. Spread the sauce across a small serving dish with the back of a spoon.
2. In a large skillet, dry toast the almonds over medium-high heat, stirring for 5–8 minutes or until they have some brown highlights and are fragrant. Don't leave unattended or stop stirring, as nuts can burn very quickly. Transfer to a small bowl.
3. Carefully wipe down the hot pan with a clean, dry kitchen towel, then place it back over a medium-high heat. Add the olive oil and, once hot, fry the broccolini on one side for 30 seconds before flipping with tongs and charring lightly on all sides so it has golden and brown highlights (about 3 minutes). Add the water to the pan and cover with a lid for 1 minute; the steam will soften the broccolini slightly. Remove the lid, sprinkle with the salt and pepper and allow any excess water to cook off.
4. Arrange the broccolini on the lemon tahini sauce and top with the toasted almonds. Serve with lemon wedges to squeeze over the broccolini.

So quick to make but the sauce and almonds made it feel extra special. The sauce was delicious and I will think of other ways to use it because I liked it that much! – Kate

Mushroom lovers, this one is for you. This rich, creamy soup made with dried porcini, portobello and button mushrooms and coconut cream is warming and hearty, perfect for a cozy winter night.

Cream of Mushroom Soup

TOTAL TIME: 45 MINUTES
SERVES 4

2 cups (1 ounce/30g) dried porcini mushrooms
2 tbsp olive oil
1 onion, finely diced
½ tsp salt
¼ tsp cracked black pepper
2 garlic cloves, crushed
2 tsp dried thyme (or substitute fresh)
2 bay leaves
1 pound (450g) portobello mushroom, sliced
1 pound (450g) white button mushrooms, sliced
6 tsp white miso paste
1 cup vegetable stock
½ cup dry white wine
¾ cup (200ml) unsweetened coconut cream
fresh thyme or parsley to garnish

1. Put the dried porcini mushrooms in a medium bowl and cover with 1 cup of boiling water. Leave to rehydrate for 20 minutes.
2. Put the olive oil in a large saucepan over medium heat and fry the onion with the salt and black pepper for 2 minutes, stirring. Add the garlic, thyme and bay leaves and stir for 1 minute. Add the portobello and button mushrooms and sauté on medium-high for 10 minutes. Remove roughly two-thirds of the mushroom mixture from the pot and set aside.
3. Mix the miso paste with the vegetable stock until dissolved, then add to the saucepan along with the white wine. Bring to a simmer then reduce the heat to low. Drain the rehydrated porcini mushrooms through a fine sieve over the saucepan, so the soaking liquid is added directly to the soup. Finely chop the rehydrated porcini mushrooms, then add those to the saucepan as well. If you prefer an extra smooth soup, at this point you can remove the bay leaves and blitz with a handheld blender.
4. Return most of the reserved mushrooms to the soup, setting aside a few for garnish. Stir in the coconut cream and, once the soup is hot, remove from heat. Remove bay leaves (if not already done) and taste, seasoning with more salt and pepper if desired. If you would like a thinner soup, add another splash of coconut cream.
5. Ladle the soup into bowls and top with the extra mushrooms, a drizzle of olive oil and some fresh thyme or parsley.

Super comforting. Will be making it again in the cooler months. – Fiona

Loved how simple it was to make, relatively cheap, one pot, loved the addition of the miso—great flavor, but subtle. – Hannah

Katsu sando is a Japanese sandwich typically made with pork schnitzel (katsu) in a soft white or milk bread with shredded cabbage and smoky tonkatsu sauce. This version uses my crispy Tofu Schnitzel (see page 146) and red cabbage instead of the traditional green.

Crispy Tofu Katsu Sando

TOTAL TIME: 30 MINUTES
MAKES 4

8 slices soft white bread, crusts removed, buttered
4 Tofu Schnitzels (page 146)
plant-based tonkatsu sauce (or barbecue sauce) to taste
plain salted potato chips to serve

CABBAGE SLAW
¼ cup plant-based mayonnaise, store bought or homemade (page 208)
1 tbsp lemon juice
1 tbsp pickled ginger, finely chopped
2 tsp Dijon mustard
⅛ tsp salt
2 cups finely shredded red cabbage
1 scallion, finely sliced lengthways

1. Prepare the Tofu Schnitzels.
2. For the cabbage slaw, combine the mayonnaise, lemon juice, pickled ginger, Dijon mustard and salt in a medium bowl. Add the cabbage and scallion and mix well to coat. Set aside.
3. Lay out four slices of the bread and top each with a Tofu Schnitzel, then drizzle with some tonkatsu sauce. Top with a quarter of the slaw and close the sandwiches with the remaining bread slices.
4. Cut the sandwiches in half and serve sliced-side up on a plate with chips on the side.

This classic sandwich is made vegan by using Tofu Scramble (see page 38) in place of eggs. The filling can be prepared in advance and made into sandwiches on the day for the freshest taste.

Curried Egg (Tofu) Sandwich

TOTAL TIME: 30 MINUTES
MAKES 4

1 batch Tofu Scramble (page 38)
⅓ cup plant-based mayonnaise, store bought or homemade (page 208)
2 tbsp plant-based margarine
1 tsp curry powder
2 scallions, halved lengthways then finely sliced
4 bread rolls or 8 slices of bread, buttered

1. Prepare the Tofu Scramble, then leave to cool in a large mixing bowl for 10 minutes. Add the mayonnaise, margarine, and curry powder, mashing with a fork to combine. Mix in the scallion, then taste and season with salt and pepper.
2. Spread the curried tofu mixture onto the bread rolls or slices and serve.

These pasties are an easy way to give leftover roasted vegetables a complete flavor makeover, and serving them with natural yogurt, lime, and Chili Oil (see page 206) gives a kick of heat with a fresh finish. I highly recommend using pumpkin in your roast veg mix, as it breaks down a little and makes the filling nice and creamy.

Curry Pasties with Roasted Vegetables

TOTAL TIME: 1 HOUR
MAKES 10

1¼ pounds (600g) mixed roasted vegetables
2 tbsp vegetable oil
1 small yellow onion, diced
4 garlic cloves, crushed
2 tsp finely grated fresh ginger
2 tbsp curry powder
1 tbsp garam masala
2 tsp ground cumin
1 tsp ground coriander
½ tsp ground turmeric
½ tsp salt
¼ tsp black pepper
¼ cup water
⅛ tsp vegetable bouillon powder
1 cup peas (frozen or cooked leftovers)
5 plant-based pie dough rounds, thawed
1–2 tbsp plant-based mayonnaise, store bought or homemade (page 208)
½ cup natural, unsweetened plant-based yogurt
juice of ½ lime
Chili Oil (page 206) to serve

1. Preheat the oven to 350°F (180°C). Line a large baking sheet with parchment paper.
2. If your leftover roast veggies are large, chop them into smaller chunks no bigger than about 1 inch (2–3cm).
3. Put the oil in a large skillet over high heat and sauté the onion for 2–3 minutes until translucent. Add the garlic and ginger and stir for another 1–2 minutes until fragrant. Add the spices, salt and pepper and stir for about 30 seconds. Add the water, bouillon powder, roasted vegetables and peas and stir gently to combine, being careful not to break up the vegetables too much. Bring to a simmer, then after 3–5 minutes, when the mixture has thickened to a paste, turn off the heat.
4. Lay a pie dough round on a cutting board and cut two 5½-inch (14cm) diameter circles from it by placing a bowl upside down and running a sharp knife around the edge. Place ¼ cup of curry mixture in the center of one dough round. Bring the edges of the dough up to meet at the top and press to seal, using your fingers to crimp the edge. Repeat with remaining filling and pie dough.
5. Place the pasties on the lined baking sheet and brush the tops with the mayonnaise to glaze. Bake for 35–40 minutes until the dough is golden brown. If they need more time, leave them in the oven and check every 5 minutes.
6. Leave to cool for 10 minutes. Mix the yogurt with the lime juice in a small bowl. Serve with sides of Chili Oil and lime yogurt.

This healthy riff on a classic convenience meal is flavored with zesty lemongrass, laksa curry paste and peanut butter. It's perfect for office lunch prep—just layer the ingredients in jars and store in the fridge. When you're ready to eat, pour boiling water over the top, leave it to sit for a few minutes until the noodles soften, then enjoy! This soup is cozy, filling, and fresh, perfect for workweek lunches.

Healthy Instant Noodle Soup

TOTAL TIME: 15 MINUTES
MAKES 4

7 ounces (200g) vermicelli noodles
1 pound (450g) extra firm tofu, cut into ¾-inch (2cm) cubes
1 bunch bok choy, trimmed and roughly chopped
4 scallions, finely sliced
1 stalk lemongrass, cut into 4
½ cup loosely packed cilantro leaves

STOCK PASTE

3 garlic cloves, crushed
4 tbsp smooth peanut butter
2 tbsp laksa curry paste (or yellow or red curry paste)
2 tbsp soy sauce
1 tbsp white miso paste
1 tbsp brown sugar
3 tsp vegetable bouillon powder
juice of 1 lime

1. For the stock paste, put all the ingredients in a small bowl and mix until well combined.
2. Divide the stock paste between four medium-sized jars or heatproof lunch containers, then break the vermicelli noodles into four and place into each container. Next, add a quarter of the tofu, bok choy, scallions, lemongrass, and cilantro leaves to each container. Seal the containers and keep in the fridge for up to four days until ready to use.
3. When you are ready to eat, pour enough boiling water into a container so that the ingredients are covered. Leave to sit for 3–5 minutes before stirring gently until the stock paste is dissolved. Eat immediately!

WECK

When I was sixteen, long before I was vegan, I did a high school exchange in France. The trip completely changed my perspective on food: no longer were meals a functional chore but rather a daily ritual to be savored and shared with others. Returning home for lunch in the middle of the school day for a sit-down meal with my host parents, and three or four courses as a standard weeknight dinner, gave me a new appreciation for the everyday pleasure of food, elevating the routine and the meal before me. Tapenade is a rich, briny and bold French spread originating in Provence. This vibrant green kale version is a plant-based twist made with capers, green olives, pine nuts, olive oil and garlic. Traditionally tapenade will sometimes include anchovies, but the briny flavor of capers and olives makes omitting them easily forgiven. Spread on a toasted baguette or crostini for a flavor-packed appetizer, or use as a topping on hummus, roast vegetables, pasta or soup. Guaranteed to add a zesty, punchy flavor hit however you enjoy it.

Kale Tapenade

TOTAL TIME: 15 MINUTES
SERVES 6

2 cups packed kale leaves, stems removed
½ cup green olives, pitted
¼ cup pine nuts, toasted
2 garlic cloves
2 tbsp capers
¼ cup extra-virgin olive oil
juice of 1 lemon
toasted baguette or crostini to serve

1. Place all the ingredients in a blender and pulse until the tapenade is chopped and combined. You can leave this on the chunkier side if you prefer or pulse a few more times for a smoother paste. Taste and add salt and pepper if desired.
2. Serve on a toasted baguette or crostini. Store any leftovers in an airtight container in the refrigerator for up to 3 days.

One of my favorite comfort foods, this classic hot snack is perfect for a lazy evening on the couch. These loaded nachos don't skimp on the toppings, either, with a textured vegetable protein crumble, sour cream, smoky Nacho Cheese Sauce (see page 18) and fresh pico de gallo salsa. It can take a little time to prep all the components, but they outshine store-bought options any day.

Loaded Nachos

TOTAL TIME: 1 HOUR
SERVES 4

½ cup textured vegetable protein
½ tsp plant-based beef bouillon powder
1 cup boiling water
1 tbsp olive oil
1 yellow onion, finely diced
4 garlic cloves, crushed
1 tbsp smoked paprika
½ tsp dried oregano
2 tsp ground cumin
½ tsp dried chili powder (optional)
1 (14-ounce/400g) can black beans, drained and rinsed
1 cup water
1 tbsp soy sauce
9½ cups (250g) corn tortilla chips
1 batch Nacho Cheese Sauce (page 18)
plant-based sour cream, store-bought or homemade (page 24)
sliced pickled jalapeños to serve
cilantro leaves to garnish

PICO DE GALLO
1 avocado, diced
2 tomatoes, diced
¼ red onion, finely diced
1 tbsp lime juice

1. Preheat the oven to 350°F (180°C).
2. Put the textured vegetable protein (TVP) in a medium-sized bowl with the bouillon powder and boiling water. Stir, then set aside to absorb for 5 minutes.
3. Heat the oil in a large skillet over medium heat and fry the onion for 2–3 minutes until translucent. Add the rehydrated TVP, garlic, smoked paprika, oregano, cumin and chili powder (if using) and cook, stirring, for 3 minutes. Add the black beans, water and soy sauce and simmer for 5–7 minutes until reduced to a thick, rich sauce. Taste and season with salt if desired.
4. To make the pico de gallo, place all the ingredients in a small mixing bowl and stir gently to combine. Set aside.
5. Arrange the corn chips on a large oven-safe serving dish and toast in the oven for 5 minutes until lightly fragrant. Top with half the Nacho Cheese Sauce then all of the TVP black bean mixture. Finish with remaining cheese sauce, pico de gallo, a dollop of sour cream, sliced pickled jalapeños, and cilantro leaves.

A delicious savory spread inspired by my memories of Christmas and picnics in France, where this would be generously slathered onto a baguette. It has the rich, earthy umami flavors of mushrooms and pine nuts. Perfect on a sandwich or as an appetizer on special occasions.

Using a food processor is not essential in this recipe, but it will give a smoother texture. Made without a food processor, the pâté will be a little lumpier but still totally delicious—call it rustic and enjoy.

Mushroom Pâté

TOTAL TIME: 30 MINUTES + 4 HOURS CHILLING TIME
SERVES 12

1 medium yellow onion
3 garlic cloves
1 pound (450g) portobello mushrooms
1 tsp white miso paste
1 tsp plant-based beef or vegetable bouillon powder
1¼ cups hot water
½ cup nutritional yeast
1½ cups panko breadcrumbs
2 tbsp olive oil
⅔ cup (80g) pine nuts
1 tsp fresh thyme leaves (or substitute dried)
juice of ½ lemon
1 tbsp soy sauce
2 tbsp (30g) plant-based butter or margarine

1. If using a food processor, roughly chop the onion and garlic, then pulse in the processor until finely chopped and remove to a bowl. Trim the dry ends of the mushroom stems, then roughly chop the rest and pulse in the processor until minced.
2. To make without a food processor, crush the garlic and very finely chop or grate the onion. Trim the dry ends of the mushroom stems, then chop the rest as finely as possible.
3. In a glass measuring cup, dissolve the miso paste and bouillon powder in the hot water. Combine the nutritional yeast and breadcrumbs in a medium bowl then pour over the miso–stock mixture and set aside to absorb.
4. Heat the olive oil in a large saucepan over medium heat and sauté the onion and garlic for 2–3 minutes until onion is translucent. Roughly chop the pine nuts and then add to the pan and cook for another 2 minutes, stirring frequently. Add the mushrooms and thyme and cook for another 3–5 minutes until the mushrooms have completely softened. Add the soaked breadcrumb mixture, lemon juice and soy sauce to the pan and mix well, continuing to cook over a gentle heat until no liquid remains.
5. For a smooth finish, add the cooked pâté mixture to a food processor and pulse until smooth, stopping to scrape down the sides as needed. If your food processor is struggling, add the tiniest splash of water and loosen the mixture with a spoon before resuming. Continue until you have reached a mostly smooth consistency (small lumps are fine).
6. Taste and season the pâté with salt and pepper as desired, then spoon the pâté into a large jar or small serving dish. Melt the butter and pour over the top, then cover and refrigerate until firm (at least 4 hours).
7. Serve as an appetizer with crostini or use as a sandwich filling. It will keep in the fridge for about five days.

It's very tasty! A nice, light option for a dip or spread. I feel like meat-eaters would even appreciate this as a lighter option to a traditional pâté. Impressive results for a beginner-level recipe—would be great for someone new to cooking or hosting wanting to make something they can be proud to serve. – Naomi

These cute little tarts look sophisticated but are so easy to make, great for a light lunch or appetizer. Flaky puff pastry contrasts well in both color and texture to the pop of juicy cherry tomatoes.

Tomato Tarts with Basil Pesto

TOTAL TIME: 35 MINUTES
MAKES 12

- 2 pints (750g) cherry or grape tomatoes
- 3 tbsp olive oil
- 2 garlic cloves, crushed
- ½ tsp salt
- 3 sheets plant-based puff pastry, thawed
- 1 batch Basil Pesto (page 196)
- plant-based feta, store bought or homemade (page 30), to serve
- balsamic glaze to serve

1. Preheat the oven to 425°F (220°C) and line a large baking sheet with parchment paper.
2. Put the tomatoes, olive oil, garlic and salt in a bowl and mix to coat the tomatoes evenly.
3. Slice the pastry sheets into quarters and place on the lined baking sheet. Spread about a tablespoon of pesto over each, leaving about a ¾-inch (2cm) border. Top each square with a few tomatoes, then fold the edges in about 1 inch (2½cm), pressing down firmly in the corners.
4. Bake for 25 minutes, rotating the baking sheet halfway through so they color evenly. The pastry should be golden and crispy. Ovens vary, so if they still look pale, leave them in for a little longer, checking every couple of minutes.
5. Top with some feta and a drizzle of balsamic glaze.

NOTES

Did you know that many store-bought pastry sheets are vegan friendly? Unless they call out "butter" on the front of the packaging, they are typically made with vegetable oil. Always check the ingredients list to be sure, as recipes can change.

Roasted cabbage is one of the most underrated roast veggies—something magical happens in the oven and this once crunchy, grassy and slightly bitter vegetable transforms into a sweet, caramelized, buttery delight with slightly charred, crispy edges. It's perfect as a side dish, with noodles, or as a salad or buddha bowl.

Roasted Red Cabbage with Peanut Sauce

TOTAL TIME: 1 HOUR
SERVES 4

½ medium head red cabbage (approx. 1¼ pounds/600g)
1 tbsp olive oil
½ tsp salt
cilantro leaves to serve

PEANUT SAUCE
½ cup smooth peanut butter
¼ cup water
juice of ½ lime
2 tbsp soy sauce
1 tsp grated fresh ginger
2 garlic cloves, crushed
¼ tsp smoked paprika

1. Preheat the oven to 425°F (220°C).
2. Remove any tough or damaged outer leaves from the cabbage. Slice into quarters through the stem so you have four wedges. Place on a baking sheet and coat with the olive oil and salt. Roast for 45 minutes until the edges are crispy and charred and the cabbage is tender.
3. Put the peanut sauce ingredients in a serving dish or small bowl and mix well.
4. Once the cabbage is done, serve immediately with peanut sauce drizzled over the top and garnish with cilantro leaves.

Simple, and it introduced me to roasted cabbage! I had only made a lime slaw for tacos using cabbage before and I was excited to try this. It used a sauce I know I love on something new. – Sarah

I first tried this classic American-style soup in Denver on a family trip back in 2012, well before my vegan days, when I was first introduced to the surprisingly balanced American lunch option of a soup and half sandwich. This plant-based version is just as comforting and can be made creamy with optional added coconut cream. Make it extra satisfying and authentic by serving it with a grilled cheese. Dunk that sandwich and enjoy!

Roasted Tomato and Basil Soup

TOTAL TIME: 50 MINUTES
SERVES 6

2¾ pounds (1.2kg) vine tomatoes
8 unpeeled garlic cloves
2 tbsp olive oil
2 yellow onions, thinly sliced
1 cup water
½ tsp vegetable bouillon powder
½ cup loosely packed basil leaves
¾ cup (200ml) unsweetened coconut cream (optional)

TO SERVE

coconut cream or natural, unsweetened plant-based yogurt
basil leaves, torn
grilled cheese sandwiches

1. Preheat the oven to 400°F (200°C).
2. Place the unpeeled garlic cloves and whole tomatoes, still on the vine, in a large roasting pan. Coat with 1 tablespoon of the olive oil and season with salt and pepper. Roast for 25–30 minutes until the tomatoes are bursting and blistered.
3. While the tomatoes are roasting, caramelize the onions. In a large saucepan, heat the remaining tablespoon of olive oil over medium-low heat. Add the onion and stir to coat, then leave to caramelize, stirring only occasionally every few minutes to avoid burning. Once the onions are a deep golden color (about 20 minutes), take them off the heat.
4. When the tomatoes and garlic are roasted, remove the vine from the tomatoes and peel the garlic cloves, being careful not to burn your fingers. Add the tomatoes and garlic to the onions along with the water, bouillon powder and basil. Blitz with a handheld blender until smooth, then place over medium heat and simmer for 10 minutes. Take off the heat and taste, seasoning with salt and pepper as required. If you'd prefer a creamier soup, add the coconut cream and stir.
5. Ladle the soup into bowls, then garnish with a drizzle of coconut cream or yogurt and basil leaves. Serve with a grilled cheese sandwich on the side.

Delicious; didn't take too long to make. Creamy but not too rich, which I find some soups can be with cream added. My partner said it was divine! – Alice

It was delicious and creamy! I loved how simple it was to make and that it had very little prep! – Clare

This classic sandwich is the perfect balance of savory, rich, and fresh flavors. I make a big platter if we are hosting a group. You can make the pesto and roast your veggies a day in advance, then build the sandwiches when you're ready to serve.

Roasted Vegetable Sandwich with Pesto

TOTAL TIME: 1 HOUR
MAKES 4

- 1 medium butternut squash, halved lengthways and seeds and skin removed, then cut into about ½-inch (1½cm) thick slices
- 1 tbsp olive oil
- ½ tsp salt
- 2 medium zucchinis, sliced about ½-inch (1½cm) thick
- ⅓ cup pitted kalamata olives, sliced in half lengthways
- ⅓ cup roasted red pepper in oil, sliced into strips
- 1 batch Basil Pesto (page 196)
- 4 bread rolls or 8 slices of fresh bread, buttered
- plant-based mayonnaise, store bought or homemade (page 208)
- large handful of arugula

1. Preheat the oven to 400°F (200°C).
2. Place the squash in a single layer on a large lined baking sheet and coat with half the olive oil and half the salt. Place the zucchini on a separate lined baking sheet and coat with the remaining olive oil and salt. Roast the squash for 25–30 minutes or until it has golden brown edges and is tender when pierced with a fork. Roast the zucchini for 10–15 minutes until tender with golden highlights.
3. When the vegetables are cooked, leave to cool for 10 minutes, then transfer to a plate lined with paper towel to absorb excess oil. Pat with a clean paper towel to absorb as much excess moisture as possible. Place the roasted pepper strips and olives on paper towel as well to absorb excess oil.
4. Spread a generous amount of pesto on one side of the rolls or bread and mayonnaise on the other. Build the sandwiches with arugula, roasted pepper strips, olives, zucchini and squash. Serve immediately.

If you love salt and vinegar chips then these are a must try. They taste like a wicked combination of potato chips and roast dinner. Serve with mayonnaise or aioli for a creamy finish to balance out the acidity.

Salt and Vinegar Roast Potatoes

TOTAL TIME: 1 HOUR 10 MINUTES
SERVES 4

2¼ pounds (1kg) white potatoes
1½ cups distilled white vinegar
1 tbsp salt
1 tbsp olive oil
plant-based aioli or mayonnaise, store bought or homemade (page 208), to serve

1. Preheat the oven to 400°F (200°C).
2. Peel the potatoes and cut into bite-size pieces of roughly 1¼ inches (3cm). (It's important they are small so the flavor can infuse.) Place the potatoes, vinegar and salt in a large saucepan and fill with water to about 1½ inches (4cm) above the potatoes.
3. Bring to a boil uncovered and continue boiling for 15–20 minutes or until the potatoes are soft. Drain and transfer to a large roasting pan lined with parchment paper. Coat with the olive oil and a large pinch of salt, then roast in the oven. After 20 minutes, turn the potatoes then continue roasting for another 20 minutes or until golden and crispy.
4. Serve immediately with mayonnaise or aioli as a side or snack.

Simple and convenient. It was delicious, something simple that I'd never thought to make. Perfect side dish! (We love potatoes.) – Fiona

It was a new flavor for roasted potatoes, and I really liked the texture of the potatoes because you boil them before baking. Great and easy recipe! – Nuša

A classic Aussie snack made plant-based with textured vegetable protein. This is very easy to make, and the fragrant additions of ground fennel seeds and apple make it more special than your standard store-bought sausage roll.

Sausage Rolls

TOTAL TIME: 1 HOUR + 20 MINUTES CHILLING TIME
MAKES 18

- 1 cup textured vegetable protein
- 1 tsp vegan beef bouillon powder
- 1 cup boiling water
- 2 tbsp olive oil
- ½ yellow onion, finely diced
- 2 garlic cloves, crushed
- 2 celery stalks, halved lengthways and finely sliced
- ½ tsp salt
- ¼ cup nutritional yeast
- 1 tsp ground fennel seeds
- 2 tbsp all-purpose flour
- 1 tsp Dijon mustard
- 1 small Granny Smith apple, peeled and finely diced (about ½ cup)
- ½ cup panko breadcrumbs
- 1 sheet plant-based puff pastry, thawed
- 1 tbsp plant-based mayonnaise, store bought or homemade (page 208)
- sesame seeds or dried oregano to garnish
- tomato relish or ketchup to serve

1. Preheat the oven to 350°F (180°C).
2. Put the textured vegetable protein (TVP), bouillon powder and boiling water in a bowl. Set aside to rehydrate for 5 minutes.
3. Heat the olive oil in a small skillet over medium heat and sauté the onion, garlic and celery for 2–3 minutes. Add the rehydrated TVP, salt, nutritional yeast, ground fennel seeds and flour and stir for another 2 minutes; the mixture should thicken and begin to form a dough ball. Turn off the heat and transfer the TVP mixture to a medium bowl. Add the Dijon mustard, apple and breadcrumbs and mix well to combine. Place the bowl in the refrigerator to chill for 20 minutes or until lukewarm.
4. Slice the puff pastry sheet in half. Place half the cooled filling along the center of one half and shape it into a log, ensuring it is well compacted. Brush the long edges of the pastry lightly with some of the mayonnaise. Fold one long edge over the filling, then roll the log and carefully press the seam so it holds together. Repeat for the second pastry half and slice both logs into rolls approximately 1½ inches (4cm) long.
5. Place the rolls on a lined baking sheet, seam side facing down, and brush the tops with the remaining mayonnaise, then sprinkle each with a pinch of sesame seeds or oregano. Bake for 35–40 minutes until golden and crispy.
6. Serve immediately with tomato relish or ketchup.

If you've never had shredded tofu before, this would be the recipe I recommend you try first. It tastes surprisingly like shredded chicken when well-seasoned, and this is a twist on a classic chicken mayo sandwich filling. It has a little crunch and lots of dill, and it tastes great the next day when stored separately from the bread.

Shredded Tofu and Mayo Sandwich

TOTAL TIME: 30 MINUTES
MAKES 6

1 pound (450g) extra firm tofu
1 tbsp olive oil
2 tbsp soy sauce
½ cup plant-based mayonnaise, store bought or homemade (page 208)
2 tsp Dijon mustard
1 tbsp lemon juice
½ tsp vegetable bouillon powder
2 celery stalks, sliced into four lengthways then finely diced
¼ small red onion, very finely diced
¼ cup loosely packed dill, finely chopped
6 bread rolls or 12 slices of bread

1. Use a vegetable grater to shred the tofu.
2. Heat the olive oil in a large skillet over medium-high heat, then add the tofu and stir for 4–5 minutes until it starts to get golden highlights. Add the soy sauce and stir for another 3–5 minutes until it is completely absorbed. Transfer to a plate to cool.
3. Put the mayonnaise, Dijon mustard, lemon juice and bouillon powder in a small bowl and mix well to combine.
4. In a large mixing bowl, combine the cooled tofu with the celery, red onion, dill and mayonnaise mixture. Mix well, then taste and season with salt and pepper as desired.
5. Butter the bread rolls or slices, then fill and serve immediately.

Easy, handy, useful for sandwiches, quick, protein-rich. I loved this recipe and will use it for sandwiches going forward. – Katia

Texturally I thought it was really great with the crunchy celery. It was a tasty sandwich. Yum! I also like how easy it was to prepare and how versatile it can be. . . . The following day I used the leftovers as a dip for crackers. – Mary-Ann

This simple but wholesome plant-based pea soup is filling, savory and punchy when topped with zesty Basil Pesto (see page 196). It may seem like too much liquid at first, but the peas thicken up a lot as it cools after cooking. This recipe makes a big batch—you can keep the leftovers in the fridge for up to three days and it is also freezer-friendly. Leftovers will thicken overnight but can be loosened with a splash of water the next day.

Hearty Yellow Split Pea Soup with Basil Pesto

TOTAL TIME: 50 MINUTES
SERVES 8

2 tbsp extra-virgin olive oil
2 yellow onions, diced
4 garlic cloves, crushed
2½ cups (500g) dried yellow split peas, rinsed well
8 cups (2L) vegetable stock
1 (13.5-ounce/400ml) can coconut milk
Basil Pesto (page 196) to serve
sourdough bread to serve

1. Heat the oil in a large saucepan over medium heat and fry the onion for 2–3 minutes until translucent. Add the garlic and stir for another minute.
2. Add the split peas and stock, increase the heat to high and bring to a boil. Reduce the heat and simmer for 25–30 minutes until the peas are tender. Taste and season with salt and pepper, then add the coconut milk and turn off the heat.
3. If you prefer a smooth soup, you can puree it at this point with a handheld blender. If you prefer a little more texture, leave it as is.
4. Serve in bowls and top with a dollop of pesto and a side of crusty sourdough.

Pesto was really nice and fresh. For such simple ingredients the soup was nice and velvety and surprisingly flavorful. It was incredibly simple and easy to make—while it takes "50 minutes," the actual work time is only around 5–10 min to get it all done. Would make a very easy winter mid-week meal. – Georgia

It was easy to make, and pretty inexpensive. The pesto is AMAZING and absolutely makes the soup. The end result is creamy but does not feel heavy. – Kaitlyn

Main

Meals

Lasagna is one of my all-time favorite childhood meals, a regular recipe in my dad's dinner repertoire. It was a classic version and nothing fancy—beef ragu, bechamel, dry pasta sheets and cheese. But the finished result was so satisfying: very cheesy, a little crispy on the edges, with a rich, meaty red sauce. At nineteen I left home for university in Melbourne and would make a big tray of lasagna in my shared house kitchen and freeze individual portions for my dinners. Even after being frozen and microwaved to high hell, I loved it. (I've never had the patience to use anything other than high power on the microwave, let alone a defrost setting.)

After going vegan, I tried a few lasagna recipes that called for cashew-based sauces or store-bought vegan cheese. I never found a recipe I liked—they were either very expensive or the cheese sauce would turn cakey and dry. I wasn't sure if I could make a version that would live up to my lofty memories of a classic beef lasagna but put it on my wish list of dream recipes. I aim to provide alternatives to popular classics that impress anybody, not just plant-based people, and here we are! This lasagna is one of the most tested recipes in this book and one that I am most proud of. I promise this recipe is worth the time.

Classic Beef Lasagna

TOTAL TIME: 2 HOURS 45 MINUTES
SERVES 8

- 3 cups (200g) textured vegetable protein
- 3 tsp vegan beef bouillon powder
- 2 cups boiling water
- 2 tbsp olive oil
- 1 onion, finely diced
- 1 celery stalk, finely diced
- 1 small carrot, finely grated
- 3 garlic cloves, crushed
- ¼ cup tomato paste
- 1 tsp dried basil
- 1 tsp dried oregano
- 1 tsp dried thyme
- 1 tsp dried parsley
- 2 bay leaves
- 1 (28-ounce/800g) can crushed tomatoes
- 3 cups (700g) tomato passata
- ¼ cup dry red wine
- 2 tbsp soy sauce
- 2 tbsp balsamic vinegar
- 2 cups water
- ½ (1-pound/500g) box dried lasagna sheets
- olive oil spray
- extra dried oregano to garnish

BECHAMEL SAUCE

- ½ cup olive oil
- ½ cup all-purpose flour
- 1½ cups nutritional yeast
- 1 tbsp vegetable bouillon powder
- 3½ cups unsweetened soy milk

1. Put the textured vegetable protein (TVP) in a medium bowl with the bouillon powder, pour the boiling water over the top and set aside for 5 minutes to absorb.
2. Add the olive oil to a large deep skillet over medium heat and sauté the onion, celery, and carrot for 5–7 minutes until the onion is translucent. Add the garlic and sauté for another minute. Add the tomato paste and sauté for an additional minute, then do the same with the herbs. Add the rehydrated TVP, crushed tomatoes, passata, red wine, soy sauce, balsamic vinegar and water. Stir to combine, then cover with a lid and cook for 30 minutes, stirring occasionally. After 30 minutes, remove the lid and reduce the heat to low, then simmer gently for 60–70 minutes, stirring occasionally. The sauce should have thickened and have a rich tomato taste. Season with salt and pepper.
3. For the bechamel sauce, heat the olive oil in a large saucepan over medium heat. Reduce the heat to low then add the flour, whisking continuously for 2 minutes. Add the nutritional yeast and bouillon powder and whisk to combine. Gradually add the soy milk, whisking continuously to avoid lumps. Increase the heat to medium and bring to a simmer, whisking occasionally for 5–8 minutes. The finished sauce should be smooth and very thick. Coat the back of a spoon with the sauce and run your finger through it: it should leave a clear line. Remove from heat when ready.
4. Preheat the oven to 400°F (200°C).
5. To assemble, spread a quarter of the TVP ragu sauce over the base of a baking dish measuring approximately 13 × 9 (32 × 24cm) and place two or three lasagna sheets on top to cover, breaking them if necessary to fit the dish. Pour a third of the bechamel sauce over the pasta sheets, then spoon over another quarter of the ragu. Repeat until there are three layers of lasagna sheets. Once you have added the final pasta layer, top it with the rest of the ragu and then pour over the bechamel. Bake in the oven for 50 minutes.
6. To finish the lasagna, spray it with olive oil and sprinkle with a small pinch of salt. Change the oven setting to broil and return the lasagna to the rack closest to the broiler until the top is golden. Broilers vary, so keep a close eye on it so it doesn't burn. It can take anywhere from 2–10 minutes.
7. Remove from the broiler and garnish with dried oregano. Let stand for at least 15 minutes to firm up before slicing.

NOTES

True to the original, this lasagna freezes well. Store in the freezer in an airtight container for up to two months. It will also keep well in the fridge for up to three days.

High protein, easy to assemble. Comfort food. – Kate

These French-inspired butter beans in a mustard sauce are creamy, hearty, and filling. The flavors of Dijon mustard, white wine and thyme are quintessentially français *and delicately balanced. Serve with a crusty baguette to mop up the sauce for a rustic vibe and cozy meal.*

Butter Beans à la Moutarde

TOTAL TIME: 35 MINUTES
SERVES 4

3 tbsp plant-based butter or margarine
2 onions, finely diced
2 garlic cloves, crushed
½ tsp salt
¼ tsp cracked black pepper
3 tbsp Dijon mustard
2 tbsp wholegrain mustard
½ cup nutritional yeast
1 tbsp dried thyme leaves
1 cup vegetable stock
½ cup dry white wine
2 (14-ounce/400g) cans butter beans, drained and rinsed
1 cup unsweetened plant-based milk
fresh parsley or thyme sprigs to serve
olive oil to serve

1. Heat the butter or margarine in a large skillet over medium heat and sauté the onion for 2–3 minutes. Reduce the heat to low and add the garlic, stirring for another minute. Add the salt, pepper, Dijon mustard, wholegrain mustard, nutritional yeast and dried thyme and stir well to form a paste. Gradually add the stock and white wine. Whisk constantly to avoid lumps. Stir in the butter beans and then simmer for 10 minutes.
2. After 10 minutes, gradually add the milk, whisking to combine. Simmer for another 10 minutes or until the sauce has thickened to the desired consistency. Taste and add extra salt and pepper as desired.
3. Ladle into bowls. Garnish with fresh parsley or thyme sprigs and a drizzle of olive oil. Serve with a crusty baguette on the side to mop up the sauce.

NOTES

Can't find butter beans? Try this with any other white bean like cannellini or white navy beans.

This is a creamy plant-based take on the classic Indian dish butter chicken. Mildly spiced and made with coconut cream instead of dairy, it is still very filling and rich. The recipe list may look daunting but I promise that this is a low-effort meal! Once you've got all your spices measured out, it comes together very quickly. Plus, it only uses one pot (yay for minimal cleaning) and is ready in half an hour.

Butter Chickpeas

TOTAL TIME: 30 MINUTES
SERVES 4

2 tbsp vegetable oil
3 garlic cloves, crushed
2 tsp finely grated fresh ginger
2 (14-ounce/400g) cans chickpeas, drained and rinsed
1 (13.5-ounce/400ml) can unsweetened coconut cream
1 cup tomato passata
½ cup water
juice of ½ lime
1 tbsp soy sauce
2 tsp sugar

HERBS AND SPICES
1 tbsp garam masala
½ tbsp ground coriander
½ tbsp ground cumin
1 tsp ground turmeric
1 tsp onion powder
½ tsp cayenne pepper (optional)
1 tsp vegetable bouillon powder (or salt)
2 bay leaves
1 tsp kasoori methi (dried fenugreek leaves)

TO SERVE
cooked basmati rice
naan or roti bread
lime wedges
fresh cilantro leaves

1. Heat the vegetable oil in a large skillet over medium heat. Add the garlic and ginger, stirring constantly for 1 minute. Add all the herbs and spices plus the chickpeas and stir for 2 minutes. If the spices begin to stick to the pan, add a splash of water. Add the coconut cream, passata, water, lime juice, soy sauce and sugar. Reduce the heat to low and simmer for 15 minutes or until thickened to desired consistency. Taste and add salt if desired.
2. Serve immediately over basmati rice with naan or roti and a wedge of lime. Garnish with fresh cilantro leaves.

NOTES

Kasoori methi can be found at South Asian grocers or online. If unavailable where you live, leave it out and the dish will still be very tasty. But I highly recommend picking some up if you can—it adds an earthy, satisfying depth of flavor.

It was so simple, and you get great flavor pay-off for minimal effort. The sauce was a perfect balance of flavors right away—I find often with curries I have to taste and adjust, but I didn't with this recipe! Also, it was so quick to make—it helped that there were no onions. I do love onions, but dicing them can take a while for me. The fact that this was just ginger and garlic definitely made it quicker! – Zara

This gratin is a creamy, hearty vegetable bake with a crispy panko-crumb topping, one of a few French-inspired dishes you'll see scattered throughout this book. I love to re-create French recipes, as they remind me of the meals my host mother made during a high school exchange. Veganizing classic recipes can be challenging, as French cuisine is synonymous with cheese, butter and meat. Still, I think I've managed to replicate the perfect balance of cheesy flavors in this gratin.

Save this one for a cold winter's night when you need something satisfying and filling. It is lovely served alongside buttery oakleaf lettuce with a simple vinaigrette. It also goes well with blanched green beans.

Cauliflower and Cannellini Bean Gratin

TOTAL TIME: 1 HOUR 15 MINUTES
SERVES 4

1 small head of cauliflower (about 2¼ pounds/600g)
4 large russet potatoes, peeled and cut into bite-size pieces (about 1¼ inches/3cm)
3 tbsp olive oil
3 tbsp (40g) plant-based butter or margarine
1 large yellow onion, halved and sliced
3 garlic cloves, crushed
½ tsp vegetable bouillon powder
¼ cup Dijon mustard
½ cup nutritional yeast
2½ cups unsweetened plant-based milk
1 (14-ounce/400g) can cannellini beans, drained and rinsed

SPICE MIX

1 tsp ground cumin
¼ tsp cayenne pepper
1 tsp salt
¼ tsp cracked black pepper
1 tsp smoked paprika
½ tsp garlic powder
½ tsp ground coriander

CRUMB TOPPING

1 cup panko breadcrumbs
2 tsp fresh thyme leaves (or substitute dried)
½ tsp salt
3 tbsp olive oil
½ tsp red pepper flakes (optional)

1. Preheat the oven to 400°F (200°C).
2. Break the cauliflower into florets. Trim away any long stems and chop into bite-size chunks.
3. Combine all the spice mix ingredients in a small bowl. Place the cauliflower on a large roasting pan and the potatoes on another. Drizzle each pan with 1 tablespoon of the olive oil, then sprinkle half the spice mix over each pan. Using your hands, massage the vegetables to coat them with the spice mix. Roast both pans for 30–35 minutes, flipping halfway through, until the potatoes and cauliflower are tender and golden.
4. In a medium bowl, combine the crumb topping ingredients and mix well.
5. Heat 1 tablespoon of the olive oil with the butter in a large saucepan over medium-high heat and sauté the onion for 2–3 minutes until translucent. Add the garlic and stir for another minute. Add the bouillon powder, mustard and nutritional yeast. Stir for 30 seconds until the mixture forms a paste. Gradually add the milk, about ¼ cup at a time, and stir constantly for 3–4 minutes until combined, smooth and free of lumps.
6. Bring the sauce to a boil over medium heat, stirring frequently. Reduce the heat to low and simmer for 3 minutes, stirring occasionally, until the sauce thickens enough to coat the back of a spoon. Remove from heat, taste and season with a pinch of salt if desired. Add the cannellini beans, roasted cauliflower and potatoes and gently mix to combine.
7. Transfer the mixture to a 10-cup (2.4L) capacity ovenproof dish (a 10-inch/25cm square or 10 × 8-inch/26 × 20cm rectangular dish both work well). Pat down the mixture so it is level, then spread the crumb topping evenly over the top. Place in the oven on the broil setting on high until the crumb is golden and crispy. Keep a very close eye on it—broilers vary, and it can burn easily! It can take anywhere from 1–7 minutes.
8. Let stand for 5 minutes before serving.

The flavor profile, textures, variety of ingredients—super yum and comforting! – Courtney

This warming pot pie is the ultimate comfort meal. It is made with roasted cauliflower, a creamy cheese-like sauce and a crispy puff pastry top. I love to serve it with green beans, carrots and roast potatoes on the side—it feels like a real farmhouse dinner.

Cheesy Cauliflower Pot Pie

TOTAL TIME: 2 HOURS
SERVES 6

1 large head of cauliflower (about 2 pounds/900g)
2 tbsp olive oil
1 tsp vegetable bouillon powder
3 tbsp plant-based butter or margarine
1 onion, finely diced
6 garlic cloves, crushed
2 bay leaves
3 tbsp miso paste
3 tbsp Dijon mustard
1 cup nutritional yeast
1 tbsp all-purpose flour
5 cups unsweetened plant-based milk
1–2 sheets plant-based puff pastry, thawed
1 tbsp plant-based mayonnaise, store bought or homemade (page 208)

1. Preheat the oven to 425°F (220°C).
2. Break the cauliflower into florets. Trim away any long stems and chop these into bite-size chunks. Place in a roasting pan and coat with the olive oil and bouillon powder, then roast for 30 minutes or until tender.
3. While the cauliflower is roasting, make the sauce. Add the butter to a large saucepan over medium heat and fry the onion for 2–3 minutes, stirring, until translucent and fragrant. Add the garlic and bay leaves and stir for another minute. Add the miso paste, Dijon mustard, nutritional yeast and flour and stir for 30 seconds until the mixture forms a paste. Gradually add the milk, whisking constantly for 3–4 minutes until combined and smooth. Bring to a boil over medium heat, stirring frequently, then reduce the heat to low and simmer for 5–7 minutes until the sauce thickens enough to coat the back of a spoon. Remove from the heat, taste and season with a pinch of salt if desired.
4. Remove the bay leaves and add the roasted cauliflower to the sauce, gently mixing to coat. Transfer this filling to a 10-cup (2.4L) capacity ovenproof dish (a 10-inch/25cm square or 10 × 8-inch/26 × 20 cm rectangular dish both work well) and chill in the refrigerator for 30 minutes. Reduce the oven temperature to 350°F (180°C).
5. Once the filling has cooled (lukewarm is fine), cover with a puff pastry sheet. If using a rectangular dish, use two sheets of pastry. Trim any excess, then press the edges down along the sides of the dish to seal. Slice a small cross in the center to allow steam to escape. If desired, use an additional sheet of puff pastry to create a decorative effect like a lattice, leaves or letters. Lightly brush the pastry top with mayonnaise.
6. Bake for 25–30 minutes or until the top is puffed and golden. Remove from the oven and rest for 5 minutes before serving.

NOTES

One of the reasons I love this recipe is that it can be made in advance, so it's a great option if you're hosting or want to stock the freezer. Simply freeze the pre-made filling, then thaw and pop a sheet of puff pastry on top when you're ready to bake! The sauce will thicken in the freeze-thaw process, so stir in an extra ¼–½ cup of milk to loosen the sauce before baking.

I am often craving a cauliflower cheese but basically no restaurants offer vegan versions. All the recipes I've tried so far were with vegan cheese (which I kind of try to avoid as it's always super processed and I'm also not a big fan of the taste) so it never tasted like a real cauliflower cheese. Your recipe is so creamy and tasty without any of the fake cheeses, and I really loved that. – Anna

Absolutely loved the flavors, and a very easy recipe. – Kerry

These baked tacos are the most satisfying combination of textures! A crispy outer shell is loaded with a rich, saucy filling and topped with a creamy, tangy Avocado Crema (see page 194) and crunchy pickled red onion and cabbage. This has to be one of my favorite recipes in this book. Made as is, the jackfruit filling is ultra-creamy and rich (which I love), but if you'd prefer a lighter option, swap the coconut cream for coconut milk. If you are short on time, you can replace the Quickle (see page 20) with finely diced red onion and the crema with diced avocado.

Baked Jackfruit and Black Bean Tacos with Avocado Crema and Quickle

TOTAL TIME: 1 HOUR
SERVES 4

2 (14-ounce/400g) cans jackfruit in brine
1 (14-ounce/400g) can black beans
1 tbsp olive oil
2 yellow onions, diced
4 garlic cloves, crushed
2 tbsp smoked paprika
2 tbsp sweet paprika
1 tbsp dried oregano
1 tbsp ground cumin
½ tsp dried chili powder (optional)
1 (13.5-ounce/400ml) can unsweetened coconut cream
4 tbsp soy sauce
8 small tortillas

TO SERVE
Avocado Crema (page 194)
Quickle (page 20)
fresh cilantro leaves
lime wedges

1. Preheat the oven to 425°F (220°C).
2. Drain and rinse the jackfruit and black beans. Shred the jackfruit by breaking the chunks apart with your hands or a fork so it is stringy.
3. Heat the olive oil in a large skillet over medium heat and sauté the onion for 2–3 minutes until translucent. Add the jackfruit and continue to stir for 3 minutes. Add the garlic, smoked paprika, sweet paprika, oregano, cumin and chili powder (if using). Cook, stirring constantly, for 2 minutes. Next add the black beans, coconut cream and soy sauce and simmer for 7–10 minutes until reduced to a thick, creamy sauce. Taste and season with salt if desired.
4. Line a large baking sheet with parchment paper. Lay the tortillas on the baking sheet and divide the filling between them, spooning onto one half. Fold the empty half over to enclose the filling and press down. Brush or spray the tacos lightly with olive oil.
5. Transfer to the oven and bake for 10–15 minutes or until the tortillas are golden and crispy.
6. Serve and top with the Avocado Crema, Quickle and cilantro leaves, plus lime wedges on the side.

NOTES

Make sure to buy unsweetened canned jackfruit in brine. Sometimes jackfruit is sold in syrup for use in sweets and desserts.

The jackfruit filling is very rich and creamy. If you'd prefer a lighter option, swap the canned coconut cream for canned coconut milk.

The crunch! Popping them in the oven was a great idea. The pickle was a great addition to cut through the richness of the avo and coconut cream mix. – Kate

Loved all components, best jackfruit recipe I've ever made. Savory, filling, and delicious! – Lia

I first came across this wickedly simple combination of hummus and gochujang on social media and was amazed at how delicious it was. Gochujang, a rich fermented chili paste from Korea, is salty and spicy with an intense umami (savory) flavor that is very enticing. What is great about gochujang is that you can use it in very simple dishes and let it do most of the heavy lifting flavor-wise. This recipe only uses a small amount of gochujang and has a medium level of heat. It's the perfect easy weeknight dinner.

Creamy Gochujang Chickpeas

TOTAL TIME: 15 MINUTES
SERVES 4

- 3 tbsp plant-based butter or margarine
- 4 garlic cloves, crushed
- 2 tbsp gochujang paste
- 2 tsp light soy sauce
- ½ cup nutritional yeast
- 2 (14-ounce/400g) cans chickpeas, drained and rinsed
- 1 cup vegetable stock
- 1 cup water
- ½ cup hummus

TO SERVE

fresh chives or scallion, lemon wedges, olive oil

1. Melt the butter or margarine in a large skillet over medium heat and sauté the garlic for 2 minutes until fragrant, then add the gochujang paste, soy sauce, nutritional yeast and chickpeas. Stir well to form a paste that coats the chickpeas. Add the vegetable stock and water and stir gently to combine. Increase the heat and bring to a boil, then reduce heat to low and simmer uncovered for 3–5 minutes until the liquid has reduced by about half.
2. Remove from the heat and stir in the hummus. Spoon into bowls and serve with chopped chives or scallions, a drizzle of olive oil and lemon wedges on the side.

If you've never heard of it before, koshari is Egypt's national dish and a popular street food. It's also probably the most deliciously savory carb-fest you'll ever try. A base of macaroni, white rice and lentils is topped with a mildly spiced tomato sauce and crispy fried onions for an extra-satisfying umami hit. You might be skeptical about this combination, but trust me, it works! As a bonus, it's budget-friendly and quick to make—perfect for feeding a crowd. Many koshari recipes take hours to make, but this version (shared with me by an Egyptian friend) is quick and just as rich.

Egyptian Koshari

TOTAL TIME: 40 MINUTES
SERVES 4

¾ cup brown lentils
¾ cup white rice
1½ cups (50g) macaroni pasta

TOMATO SAUCE
1 tbsp vegetable oil
2 garlic cloves, crushed
1 tsp za'atar (or substitute dried oregano)
1 tsp salt
¼ tsp sugar
¼ tsp ground cinnamon
¼ tsp smoked paprika
1 tbsp distilled white vinegar
½ cup (140g) tomato paste
1 (14-ounce/400g) can diced tomatoes
3½ cups (800ml) boiling water

CRISPY ONIONS
1 large yellow onion
3 tbsp all-purpose flour
½ tsp salt
¼ cup vegetable oil

1. In separate saucepans, cook the rice, lentils and macaroni in salted water according to package instructions. Arrange all three on a large platter.
2. For the tomato sauce, heat the vegetable oil in a saucepan over medium heat and fry the garlic for 1 minute before adding all the spices, sugar and vinegar. Cook for 1–2 minutes, stirring constantly to prevent the spices from burning (they will start to stick a little to the pan, but try your best). Add a splash of boiling water to deglaze the saucepan, running the spoon around the base and edges to loosen all the spices and mixing well. Add the tomato paste and tomatoes and stir until combined. Increase the heat and bring to a boil, then reduce the heat to low and simmer until the liquid has reduced by half (around 20 minutes). Taste and add more sugar if it is too sour or add salt if needed. Using a handheld blender, blitz the sauce until smooth, then transfer to a serving dish.
3. For the crispy onions, cut the onion in half and slice into thin half-rounds. Transfer to a bowl and coat with the flour and salt, using your hands if necessary. Heat the vegetable oil in a large skillet until hot. (You can test by dropping a small piece of onion into the oil—if it sizzles and bubbles around the edges, you're good to go!) Fry the onions, stirring occasionally, until golden and crispy. Spread them out on paper towel to remove any excess oil, then transfer to a small serving dish.
4. To serve, place the sauce, the crispy onions and the macaroni, rice and lentil platter in the middle of the table and allow everybody to serve themselves. Mix the macaroni, rice and lentils together on your plate and top with the sauce and onions.

Very filling and comforting—the perfect nostalgic meal that makes a large serving for a family or gathering. – Sumera

A weeknight hero, this is high in protein, medium spicy and takes only half an hour from start to finish. It's pretty much just three steps: coat tofu, pan-fry, pour sauce. Very easy, very tasty.

Gochujang Tofu

TOTAL TIME: 30 MINUTES
SERVES 4

¾ cup cornstarch
2 tsp garlic powder
2 tsp onion powder
1 tsp salt
½ tsp cracked black pepper
1¾ pounds (800g) extra firm tofu, broken into bite-size chunks
3 tbsp vegetable oil

GOCHUJANG SAUCE
3 tbsp gochujang paste
2 tbsp rice wine vinegar
½ cup water
2 tbsp soy sauce
1 tbsp sesame oil
1 tbsp vegetable oil
1 tbsp brown sugar

TO SERVE
brown rice
sliced scallions
sesame seeds

1. Prepare the gochujang sauce by whisking all the ingredients together in a small bowl until well combined.
2. In a large bowl, combine the cornstarch, garlic powder, onion powder, salt and pepper. Add the tofu to the cornstarch mixture and coat gently with your hands.
3. Heat half of the vegetable oil in a large non-stick skillet over medium-high heat. Check if the oil is hot enough by dropping in a tiny piece of tofu—it should sizzle as soon as it touches the pan. Add half the tofu to the pan (so as not to overcrowd) and pan-fry until crispy and golden. Set the first batch of tofu aside on a plate lined with paper towel, then repeat with the remaining vegetable oil and tofu.
4. Reduce the heat to low and return all the tofu to the pan. Pour the gochujang sauce over the tofu and stir gently until well coated.
5. Serve immediately on brown rice and garnish with sliced scallions and sesame seeds.

NOTES

Make this even faster by using microwave brown rice. I always keep some in the pantry and it makes life immensely easier, especially after a long day. You could also serve this over white rice (or any rice you'd like) to shorten the prep time.

As always, please make sure to use the right tofu. This recipe requires extra firm tofu (sometimes called hard tofu)—it should be dense, robust, and not at all soft or wet inside. I know they sound similar, but anything referred to as classic tofu or firm tofu will be too soft.

So simple but really tasty. I liked the method of breaking the tofu rather than cutting into cubes as you got a better surface area to go crispy and more coverage with the sauce. I thought the sauce might be too spicy, but it was just a nice mellow heat. – Georgia

A French classic, bourguignon is a rich red wine stew typically made with beef. This veggie version is just as hearty, as the mushrooms have a meaty and earthy umami flavor. Perfect for a warming winter meal, it tastes even better served the next day! It is, however, a labor of love (but trust me—it's worth the effort) and needs to be prepared a day in advance by marinating the veggies overnight. Please don't skip this step as it really gives the dish its intense flavor and it's just not the same otherwise. Serve over mashed potatoes to soak up the delicious gravy-like sauce, and for the full at-home French experience, mop your plate with a piece of torn baguette.

Mushroom Bourguignon

TOTAL TIME: 12 HOURS (INCLUDING OVERNIGHT MARINADE)
SERVES 4

12 very small onions, peeled (whole pearl onions or French shallots)
3 carrots, peeled and cut into 1¼-inch (3cm) pieces
2 bay leaves
4 sprigs thyme
1 cup dry red wine
2 cups water
1 tsp plant-based beef bouillon powder (or substitute vegetable bouillon powder)
1⅓ cups (.75 ounce/20g) dried porcini mushrooms
olive oil for cooking
11 ounces (300g) cremini mushrooms, quartered
11 ounces (300g) white button mushrooms, quartered
3 tbsp plant-based butter or margarine
1 red bell pepper, diced
4 garlic cloves, crushed
2 tbsp tomato paste
4 tbsp all-purpose flour
1 cup plant-based beef or vegetable stock
1 tbsp soy sauce

TO SERVE

mashed potatoes
fresh thyme leaves or parsley to garnish
baguette

1. Place the onions, carrots, bay leaves and thyme in a large bowl or storage container. In a large liquid measuring cup, combine the red wine, water and bouillon powder and pour over the vegetables to cover. Refrigerate covered overnight or for at least 10 hours.
2. The next day, preheat the oven to 350°F (180°C).
3. Drain the marinated vegetables, bay leaves and thyme, reserving the marinade liquid. Separate the onions, carrots, bay leaves and thyme, as they will be cooked separately.
4. Place the porcini mushrooms in a bowl and add 1 cup of hot water to rehydrate for 20 minutes.
5. Add a generous glug of olive oil to a large ovenproof pot over high heat and sauté the marinated onions for 5–7 minutes until they are slightly browned. Remove to a bowl.
6. Add more olive oil as needed, then add all the fresh mushrooms. Sauté until all their liquid is expelled, then remove from the pot and set aside with the onions.
7. Once the porcini mushrooms are rehydrated, drain and reserve the liquid (this will be added to the sauce). Finely dice the porcini.
8. Reduce the heat to medium and add the butter or margarine to the pot. Once melted, fry the carrots, bay leaves and thyme for 2–3 minutes, stirring constantly. Add the diced bell pepper and cook for 2 minutes. Add the garlic and continue stirring for 1 minute. Add the cooked onions and mushrooms plus the diced porcini to the pot. Add the tomato paste and stir for 1 minute, ensuring the vegetables are well coated. Add the flour and stir well to combine. (The flour will begin to form a paste.) Gradually add the stock, stirring constantly to ensure no lumps form, then add the reserved marinade liquid, reserved porcini liquid and soy sauce. Stir well to combine, then increase the heat to high and bring to a boil. Reduce the heat to low and simmer uncovered for 20 minutes.
9. Place the lid on the pot and transfer to the oven for 60 minutes.
10. Serve over mashed potatoes with a few extra thyme leaves to garnish and some torn baguette to mop up the sauce.

Love that it was made all in one pot. So rich and delicious, and I could absolutely serve this to my non-vegan family and friends. – Hannah

This earthy galette may look a little fancy but is so simple to make. It is perfect for easy entertaining as a light lunch. Serve with some sides like roast vegetables or simple greens to make it more substantial or slice it into small portions and serve as finger food. Don't skip the toppings of feta, arugula, and balsamic glaze for the perfect flavor balance.

Mushroom Galette

TOTAL TIME: 45 MINUTES
SERVES 4

3 tbsp olive oil
1 large yellow onion, halved and thinly sliced
1¼ pounds (600g) portobello mushrooms, sliced
2 tsp vegetable bouillon powder
¾ cup merlot or other full-bodied dry red wine
2 sheets plant-based puff pastry, thawed
1 tsp plant-based mayonnaise, store bought or homemade (page 208)

TO SERVE
plant-based feta, store bought or homemade (page 30)
arugula
balsamic glaze

1. Preheat the oven to 425°F (220°C) and line a large baking sheet with parchment paper.
2. Add the oil to a skillet over medium-high heat and fry the onion, stirring, for 3–4 minutes until translucent. Add the mushrooms, bouillon powder and red wine and simmer uncovered, stirring frequently, for around 10 minutes, until most of the liquid has reduced. Season with salt and pepper to taste.
3. Place the pastry sheets on the lined baking sheet so they overlap by about 1 inch (2½cm). Join the sheets by pressing the seam with the back of a fork.
4. Spread the mushroom filling over the pastry, leaving about a 2-inch (5cm) border all around. Fold the edges over, then lightly brush them with mayonnaise. Bake for 25 minutes until the pastry is golden brown.
5. Top with crumbled feta, arugula and a drizzle of balsamic glaze.

This rich, creamy and hearty stroganoff is the perfect cozy winter meal. Made with coconut milk instead of dairy cream and tempeh for added protein, it's easy and made with just one pot. A delicious plant-based twist on the classic beef dish that can be served over pasta or rice.

Mushroom Tempeh Stroganoff

TOTAL TIME: 45 MINUTES
SERVES 4

3 tbsp extra-virgin olive oil
11 ounces (300g) tempeh, cut into 1-inch (2½cm) cubes
2 yellow onions, finely diced
1¼ pounds (600g) white button mushrooms, quartered
7 garlic cloves, crushed
2 tsp smoked paprika
2 tsp dried thyme
2 (13.5-ounce/400ml) cans unsweetened coconut milk
2 tbsp soy sauce
2 tbsp Dijon mustard
¼ cup nutritional yeast
½ cup loosely packed parsley leaves, roughly chopped
pappardelle pasta or white rice to serve

1. Heat 2 tablespoons of the olive oil in a large skillet over medium-high heat. Once the oil is hot, fry the tempeh on all sides until lightly golden (4–6 minutes), then remove to a plate.
2. Add the remaining tablespoon of olive oil to the pan and sauté the onion for 2–3 minutes until translucent. Add the mushrooms and garlic, stir for 1 minute, then add the smoked paprika and thyme, stirring for another 1–2 minutes until fragrant. Add the coconut milk, soy sauce and mustard to the pan, stirring. Bring to a boil, then turn the heat down to low and simmer for 10–15 minutes until the sauce has reduced and thickened to the desired consistency.
3. Stir in the nutritional yeast, fried tempeh and most of the parsley, reserving some to garnish. Taste the sauce and season with pepper, salt or an extra splash of soy sauce.
4. Serve the pasta or rice in bowls and spoon the stroganoff over the top. Garnish with the remaining parsley.

These creamy noodles are a comforting, no-fuss dinner. Perfect for a Friday night after a long week with a crisp dry cider or beer.

Peanut Noodles

TOTAL TIME: 20 MINUTES
SERVES 2

1 tsp grated fresh ginger
3 garlic cloves, crushed
2 tbsp soy sauce
⅓ cup smooth peanut butter
½ tbsp sriracha hot sauce (optional)
1 tsp smoked paprika
1 tbsp vegetable oil
1 pound (450g) extra firm tofu, cut into bite-size pieces
14 ounces (400g) thick udon noodles

TO SERVE
finely sliced scallions
sesame seeds
fresh cilantro leaves

1. Combine the ginger, garlic, soy sauce, peanut butter, sriracha (if using) and smoked paprika in a small bowl and set aside.
2. Heat the oil in a large skillet over medium-high heat. Once hot, pan-fry the tofu for a couple of minutes on each side until golden.
3. Prepare the noodles according to package instructions. When draining the noodles, reserve ½ cup of the cooking water and stir that into the sauce mixture.
4. Add the fried tofu to the noodles and pour the sauce over the top, stirring to combine. Garnish with scallions, sesame seeds, and cilantro leaves.

NOTES

Want to add some veggies? These noodles are delicious with some steamed greens like bok choy, broccoli, or even wilted kale on the side.

Wholesome and filling, this simple meal pairs tangy basil pesto with buttery cannellini beans cooked in a vegetable broth. Serve with crusty sourdough toast.

Pesto Cannellini Beans

TOTAL TIME: 30 MINUTES
SERVES 4

1 tbsp olive oil
1 yellow onion, finely diced
2 (14-ounce/400g) cans cannellini beans, drained and rinsed
1 tsp vegetable bouillon powder
1 cup water

BASIL PESTO
¼ cup raw cashews
¼ cup pine nuts
2 cups loosely packed basil leaves
2 garlic cloves, roughly chopped
½ cup olive oil
½ tsp salt
juice of 1 lemon

TO SERVE
sourdough toast
lemon wedges
basil leaves to garnish
red pepper flakes or Chili Oil (page 206), optional

1. For the basil pesto, put the cashews in a large, dry skillet over medium-low heat and toast for 2 minutes, shaking the pan or stirring every 20 seconds or so. Reduce the heat to low and add the pine nuts, continuing to toast for 2–4 minutes and shaking the pan frequently to avoid burning. Remove from the heat once the nuts have golden brown highlights and are fragrant. Put the toasted nuts and the remaining pesto ingredients in a food processor or blender and blitz until mostly smooth with some small chunks of cashews remaining (about 30 seconds to 1 minute), stopping to scrape down the sides as needed. If the pesto is too thick, add an extra 1–2 tablespoons of olive oil to loosen. Set aside.
2. Heat the olive oil in a skillet over medium heat and sauté the onion for 2–3 minutes until translucent. Add the cannellini beans, bouillon powder, and water and bring to a boil, then reduce heat and simmer for 3–5 minutes until the liquid is reduced by half. Turn off the heat, add the pesto, and stir gently to combine.
3. Serve immediately in bowls with buttered sourdough toast, a wedge of lemon, fresh basil leaves, and red pepper flakes or Chili Oil (if using).

Simple to make and quick for a midweek meal . . . I loved it. – Larni

Is there anything better than a warming, nourishing dal? My version uses classic red lentils plus extra veggies in the form of roasted cauliflower and creamy sweet potato. Soupy, mildly spiced, filling, and good for the soul, this recipe makes a big batch and is freezer friendly.

You know those times when you want to help care for somebody who is having a hard time? Maybe they're unwell, have had a baby, or are just in the thick of life? This is the perfect meal to leave on their doorstep. Don't forget to add some microwavable rice to their care package too.

Roasted Cauliflower and Sweet Potato Dal

TOTAL TIME: 50 MINUTES
SERVES 6

½ medium head of cauliflower (about 14 ounces/400g), broken into florets
1 medium sweet potato, peeled, ends trimmed and cut into 1¼-inch (3cm) chunks
3 tbsp olive oil
1 red onion, diced
4 garlic cloves, crushed
2 tbsp grated fresh ginger
2 bay leaves
½ cup tomato paste
5 cups water
3 tbsp soy sauce
2 tsp vegetable bouillon powder
2 cups red lentils, rinsed
1 (13.5-ounce/400ml) can coconut milk
2½ cups (80g) loosely packed baby spinach
juice of 1 lime

SPICES
1 tbsp garam masala
2 tsp curry powder
2 tsp ground coriander
2 tsp ground turmeric
2 tsp ground cumin
¼ tsp cayenne pepper
1 tsp vegetable bouillon powder

TO SERVE
basmati rice
coconut yogurt
lime wedges
finely sliced fresh chili (optional)

1. Combine all the spices in a small bowl. Set aside.
2. Preheat the oven to 400°F (200°C). Line two large baking sheets with parchment paper.
3. Place the cauliflower and sweet potato in separate large mixing bowls. Drizzle each with 1 tablespoon of the olive oil and 2 teaspoons of the spice mix. Coat well with your hands, then spread the cauliflower and sweet potato over the two separate baking sheets and drizzle both with an extra glug of olive oil. Roast in the oven for 15 minutes, then flip. Roast the cauliflower for another 10–15 minutes (25–30 minutes in total) or until tender when pierced with a fork. Roast the sweet potato for another 20–25 minutes (35–40 minutes in total) or until soft when pierced with a fork.
4. While the vegetables are roasting, heat the remaining tablespoon of olive oil in a large saucepan over medium-high heat and sauté the onion for 2 minutes until translucent. Add the garlic, ginger, remaining spice mix and bay leaves, stirring constantly for 1 minute. Add the tomato paste, water, soy sauce, bouillon powder and lentils. Bring to a boil, then reduce the heat to medium and cook covered for 20 minutes, stirring occasionally, until the lentils are softened.
5. Remove the bay leaves and add the coconut milk and baby spinach, stirring gently for 2 minutes until the spinach has begun to wilt. Gently stir in the roasted sweet potato and cauliflower and the lime juice, then turn off the heat and taste, adding salt or extra soy sauce if desired.
6. Serve over basmati rice and top with coconut yogurt, a wedge of lime, and sliced chili (if using).

Really nice flavor, love that there are lots of veggies for robustness. – Monica

Shepherd's pie is my definition of wholesome comfort food and was a regular part of my family's dinner repertoire growing up. My recipe has just a little bit of curry powder and is crowned with a cheesy mashed potato topping. As you might have noticed, I love textured vegetable protein. It is my go-to ground beef substitute—it's high in protein, affordable, and keeps in the pantry. When combined with lentils, the texture is even more satisfying, as the soft lentils balance out the slight chewiness of the TVP.

Mildly Spiced Shepherd's Pie

TOTAL TIME: 1 HOUR 45 MINUTES
SERVES 6

¾ cup textured vegetable protein
½ tsp plant-based beef bouillon powder
1 cup boiling water
1 tbsp olive oil
1 large yellow onion, finely diced
1 large carrot, peeled and finely diced
1 celery stalk, finely sliced
2 tsp curry powder
½ tsp vegetable bouillon powder
½ tsp dried rosemary
½ tsp dried thyme
3 bay leaves
1 tbsp soy sauce
3 tbsp Worcestershire sauce
⅓ cup tomato paste
1 (14-ounce/400g) can lentils, drained and rinsed
¼ cup all-purpose flour
3 cups water
1 cup frozen peas

MASHED POTATO TOPPING

3 pounds (1.4kg) russet potatoes, peeled and cut into 1-inch (2.5cm) chunks
¼ cup unsweetened plant-based milk
¼ cup nutritional yeast
1 tbsp plant-based butter or margarine
½ tsp salt
olive oil spray

1. Preheat the oven to 350°F (180°C).
2. Put the textured vegetable protein (TVP) in a small bowl with the beef bouillon powder and cover with the boiling water. Stir, then set aside to absorb for 5 minutes.
3. Put the olive oil in a large skillet over medium heat and sauté the onion, carrot and celery for 5–7 minutes until the onion is translucent and the celery and carrot have begun to soften. Add the curry powder, vegetable bouillon powder, rosemary, thyme and bay leaves and stir for 1 minute until fragrant. Add the soy sauce, Worcestershire sauce, tomato paste, rehydrated TVP and lentils, stirring well to combine. Stir in the flour, then add the water and bring to a boil. Reduce the heat to low and simmer for 25 minutes, stirring occasionally.
4. After 25 minutes, the sauce should have a thick, gravy-like consistency. Taste and add salt and pepper if desired. Stir in the frozen peas and transfer to an 8-cup (2L) capacity baking dish. Smooth the top and set aside while you prepare the topping.
5. For the mashed potato topping, place the potatoes in a large saucepan of salted water and bring to a boil over high heat. Leave to boil for 10 minutes or until potatoes have softened and can be pierced with a fork. Drain potatoes and return them to the saucepan. Add the milk, nutritional yeast, butter and salt and mash well until smooth and no lumps remain.
6. Dollop the mashed potatoes on top of the filling and gently spread to form an even layer. Run a fork over the top of the mashed potato to add a rough finish—this will help it get nice and crispy in the oven. Lightly spray the mashed potatoes with olive oil and sprinkle a tiny pinch of salt over them if you like.
7. Bake in the oven for 30 minutes, then change the setting to broil and move to the top rack for 5–10 more minutes until the top turns golden and has brown, crispy highlights. Let stand for 10 minutes before serving.
8. Leftovers can be kept in an airtight container in the refrigerator for up to four days. This also freezes well for up to two months.

NOTES

Not a fan of TVP? Substitute an extra can of lentils and omit the cup of boiling water. Mix in the beef bouillon powder when adding the lentils.

Reminiscent of traditional shepherd's pie but even tastier. The TVP and lentils make it protein-rich. Liked the addition of nutritional yeast in the mashed potatoes so much that I may add it all the time now when I make them. – Kate

This rustic Greek pie is crispy on the outside with a creamy spinach tofu ricotta filling on the inside. It's somehow both light and very filling, with plenty of garlic and olive oil balanced by fresh parsley, dill, and lemon. The key to its signature flaky phyllo dough is to remove as much liquid as possible from the filling and brush each individual sheet with oil. This one is a labor of love but definitely worth it.

Spanakopita

TOTAL TIME: 1 HOUR 50 MINUTES
SERVES 6

SPANAKOPITA

2 tbsp extra-virgin olive oil
1 yellow onion, finely diced
4 garlic cloves, crushed
18 ounces (500g) chopped spinach (fresh or frozen)
¾ cup loosely packed parsley, finely chopped
⅓ cup loosely packed dill, finely chopped
zest of 1 lemon
¼ tsp ground nutmeg
½ tsp salt
few twists of cracked pepper
13 ounces (375g) plant-based phyllo dough, thawed
½ cup vegetable oil to brush pastry

TOFU RICOTTA

1 pound (450g) extra firm tofu
½ cup almond meal
1 tbsp hemp seeds
juice of 1 lemon
2 tbsp olive oil
2 garlic cloves
2 tsp dried basil
1½ tsp salt
¼ cup nutritional yeast
pinch of ground black pepper

1. For the tofu ricotta, first press the tofu by placing the block between sheets of paper towel or wrapping in a clean, non-fluffy tea towel and weighing it down with a cutting board and some heavy objects for 30 minutes (a cast-iron dish or pan works nicely). Crumble the pressed tofu into a food processor and add the remaining ingredients, then blitz on high for 1 minute or until well combined, stopping occasionally to scrape down the sides if needed. The finished result should be a thick, creamy, ricotta-like consistency. Some small lumps are okay.
2. Preheat the oven to 350°F (180°C).
3. Add 1 tablespoon of the olive oil to a large skillet and sauté the onion for 3–4 minutes, stirring, until it becomes translucent. Add the garlic and stir for another minute. Remove from the pan to a large mixing bowl.
4. If using fresh spinach, add the remaining tablespoon of olive oil to the pan and gradually fry the spinach, stirring until it wilts then adding more until it's all wilted. If using frozen spinach, thaw by microwaving on high for 1–2 minutes or until soft. Once cool enough to handle, take very small handfuls and squeeze out excess water. (This step is critical to ensure the phyllo is not soggy.) After you have squeezed each handful, place it on a clean kitchen towel. Once you have piled all the spinach onto the kitchen towel, wring it very tightly to squeeze as much water out as possible. Repeat this with another clean towel to really work out every last drop.
5. Break apart the compacted ball of spinach and add it to the mixing bowl with the onion and garlic. Add the parsley, dill, lemon zest, nutmeg, salt and pepper.
6. Lightly brush a 10-inch (26cm) ovenproof skillet or round baking dish with vegetable oil. Put a damp tea towel on your surface and lay the phyllo dough on top. Layer one sheet at a time in the skillet, brushing each with vegetable oil as you go, until you have about 20 sheets, rotating the placement of the sheets so the overhanging edges are evenly distributed. Try to work quickly, as the dough dries out easily. Spread the filling mixture evenly over the dough to the edges of the skillet.
7. To make the rosette topping, brush a sheet of phyllo with oil and roughly scrunch it into a loose rosette. Place on top of the filling and continue until covered, about 6–8 sheets.
8. Bake in the oven for 45 minutes or until golden, rotating partway through for even color. Let stand for 10 minutes before slicing.

NOTES

Spanakopita leftovers are also delicious served cold.

Growing up, one of my favorite take-out meals was lemon chicken from our local Chinese restaurant. I loved the combination of sweet and sour flavors. In my early twenties I was visiting a friend in the US and I discovered they don't have lemon chicken—their equivalent meal is orange chicken. *I thought it was like this funny parallel universe. Years later, after going vegan, I got a pang for lemon chicken. After a bit of testing, I ended up making a sweet orange sauce instead—it just seems to pair better with the tofu and didn't need a batter to taste amazing. I added a little chili to balance the sweetness with just a touch of heat. It's a little different but still sweet and tangy, like the original.*

Sticky Orange Tofu

TOTAL TIME: 40 MINUTES
SERVES 4

21 ounces (600g) extra firm tofu
1 tbsp cornstarch
½ tsp garlic powder
½ tsp salt
¼ tsp cracked black pepper
vegetable oil for frying
white rice to serve

ORANGE SAUCE
2 tbsp vegetable oil
1 yellow onion, diced
3 garlic cloves, crushed
1 tsp grated fresh ginger
½ tsp red pepper flakes
zest and juice of 2 large oranges
⅓ cup sugar
2 tbsp rice wine vinegar
1 tbsp soy sauce
1 cup green beans, chopped into roughly 1¼-inch (3cm) lengths
1 tbsp cornstarch, dissovled in a splash of water

1. Cut the tofu into large cubes (about 1¼ inch/3cm).
2. In a large bowl, mix the cornstarch, garlic powder, salt and pepper. Add the tofu to the bowl and use your hands to mix well and ensure all cubes are coated evenly.
3. Heat a generous glug of oil in a skillet over high heat. Add the tofu and fry on all sides until golden and crispy. Place the cooked tofu onto paper towel to absorb any excess oil and set aside.
4. For the orange sauce, heat the oil over medium heat and fry the onion for 2–3 minutes until translucent. Add the garlic, ginger and red pepper flakes, stirring constantly for 1–2 minutes. Add the orange juice, three-quarters of the orange zest, sugar, rice wine vinegar and soy sauce, stirring constantly for 2 minutes. Add the green beans and cook for another minute before adding the cornstarch mixture. Once the cornstarch is combined, add the tofu to the sauce and stir until coated.
5. Serve immediately over white rice and top with the remaining orange zest.

When I lived in America, we had a Chinese restaurant around the corner and they had orange chicken and orange beef on their menu. I used to get the chicken a lot and it was one of my favorite things ever. I stopped eating meat a long time ago, but I couldn't find any veg dishes in restaurants or recipes that taste like the one I used to like. I thought it'd be easy to just substitute the chicken with tofu but I just couldn't really find the right recipe—until this one. It's so delicious, I am absolutely obsessed with it. Thank you so much, this was so unexpected and I couldn't be happier. – Anna

If I had to pick just one cuisine to eat for the rest of my life it would be Thai. Not only is the food delicious but every time those flavors hit my lips, I'm magically transported back to memories of humid nights on holiday, flying about in a tuktuk and gorging on decadent Thai street food like khao kha moo, pad Thai or mango sticky rice. I traveled there twice in my early twenties (pre-vegan days), and it was on the second trip with my then boyfriend, now husband, that I took my first cooking class. We learned the principles of Thai cuisine and how to balance salty, sour, sweet, spicy and creamy flavors. The stand-out meal from the trip was a massaman curry on Koh Phi Phi island, which inspired this recipe. My plant-based twist is a little different from the traditional but still super creamy from coconut and peanut butter, with zesty Thai flavors like lime leaves, lime juice, and cilantro. Chickpeas replace the meat as the protein in this dish and make it dense, wholesome and filling.

Thai-Inspired Peanut Chickpea Curry

TOTAL TIME: 45 MINUTES
SERVES: 6

- 1 tbsp vegetable oil
- 1 large yellow onion, halved and sliced
- 4 garlic cloves, crushed
- 1 tbsp grated fresh ginger
- 4 tbsp massaman curry paste (I use Maesri brand)
- 2 large russet potatoes, peeled and cut into 1-inch (2½cm) chunks
- 1 large carrot, sliced into thin rounds or batons
- 2 (14-ounce/400g) cans chickpeas, drained and rinsed
- 1 cup water
- 1 cup vegetable stock
- ¼ cup smooth natural peanut butter
- 2 tbsp soy sauce
- ½ cup raw peanuts
- 2 makrut lime leaves, finely shredded
- 1 (13.5-ounce/400ml) can coconut cream
- juice of ½ lime
- 4 cups (110g) loosely packed baby spinach
- ½ cup cilantro leaves, roughly chopped

TO SERVE

- white rice
- extra peanuts
- sliced fresh red chili
- cilantro leaves
- lime wedges

NOTES

The massaman curry paste can be substituted with red curry paste if preferred.

1. Heat the oil in a large saucepan and sauté the onion for 3 minutes until translucent. Add the garlic and ginger and sauté for another minute. Add the curry paste and stir constantly for 1 minute, then add the potato, carrot, and chickpeas, stirring until coated in curry paste. Deglaze the pot with the cup of water.
2. Working quickly, combine the stock, peanut butter, and soy sauce in a small bowl and add to the pot along with the peanuts and makrut lime leaves, stirring to combine. Bring to a boil then reduce the heat and simmer for 10–15 minutes, stirring occasionally to prevent burning, until the potato and carrot have softened.
3. Add the coconut cream, lime juice, spinach, and cilantro leaves and stir to combine. After 1–2 minutes, once the spinach leaves have wilted, turn off the heat. Serve over white rice and garnish with peanuts, sliced fresh chili, cilantro, and a wedge of lime.

I grew up on a hobby farm, and although I've lived in the city for more than a decade now, I'm still a country girl at heart. Nothing speaks to my soul more than an Aussie pub meal. This crispy Tofu Schnitzel tastes surprisingly similar to the original chicken version. When I've served this to non-vegan friends, they've given me confused looks and asked what it was that they were eating—the ultimate compliment! It's great as a parmigiana, with katsu curry, or on its own with a leafy salad and a squeeze of lemon.

Tofu Schnitzel

TOTAL TIME: 25 MINUTES
SERVES 4

1 pound (450g) extra firm tofu
¼ cup soy sauce
aquafaba from 1 (14-ounce/400g) can chickpeas
¼ cup cornstarch
sunflower oil for shallow frying

CRUMB MIX
1⅔ cups (100g) panko breadcrumbs
¼ cup nutritional yeast
1 tsp smoked paprika
1 tsp vegetable bouillon powder

1. Press the tofu block by placing it between sheets of paper towel or wrapping in a clean, non-fluffy tea towel and weighing it down for 10–20 minutes with a cutting board and some heavy objects (a cast-iron dish or some cookbooks work nicely).
2. Slice the pressed tofu into four large pieces roughly ⅜-inch (1cm) thick. Lay them on a shallow dish and pour over the soy sauce to marinate while you prep the crumb mix. Flip them over after a few minutes so they absorb evenly.
3. Combine all the crumb mix ingredients in a bowl and stir to combine. Transfer to a dinner plate.
4. Drain the chickpeas and reserve the aquafaba. The chickpeas themselves are not needed for this recipe, so pop those into an airtight container in the fridge and keep for another recipe. Carefully pour the aquafaba onto a second dinner plate.
5. Place the cornstarch on a third dinner plate, then line your plates up for dipping: cornstarch, aquafaba and crumb mix.
6. Coat each schnitzel in a thin layer of cornstarch on both sides, then dip into aquafaba to form a gelatinous egg-white-like layer. Next, coat the schnitzel on both sides in the crumb mix. Sprinkle extra crumb mix over the top and press down to get it to stick well to the tofu. Give it a light shake so any excess crumb falls off, then transfer to another plate. (You can freeze the schnitzels at this point if you would like to cook them up another day.)
7. Add a generous glug of the oil to a large skillet over medium-high heat. To test if the oil is hot enough for frying, add a breadcrumb to the pan, and if it sizzles immediately, it's ready. Fry the schnitzels until golden brown on both sides—it takes about 2 minutes per side.
8. Transfer the schnitzels to a plate lined with paper towel to remove any excess oil and allow to cool slightly.
9. Serve with a green leafy salad, a wedge of lemon and mayonnaise or aioli.

Pasta

This creamy pasta is so easy to make. It's a silky-smooth blend of some classic cheesy vegan ingredients with smoky, salty tofu bacon bits that can be made three ways. Prefer a chewy, less oily bacon? Oven bake or use an air fryer. Or pan-fry for that classic, slightly oily bacon.

Cashew Carbonara with Smoky Tofu Bacon

TOTAL TIME: 35 MINUTES
SERVES 4

1 cup raw cashews
½ cup unsweetened soy milk
juice of ½ lemon
1 garlic clove
1 tbsp nutritional yeast
2 tsp white miso paste
1 pound (500g) spaghetti or other pasta of choice (cooked to package instructions) to serve

TOFU BACON BITS

1 pound (450g) extra firm tofu
⅓ cup soy sauce
1 tbsp maple syrup
1 tsp smoked paprika

1. For the tofu bacon bits, press the tofu first (if you have time) by placing the block between sheets of paper towel or wrapping in a clean, non-fluffy tea towel and weighing it down with a cutting board and some heavy objects for 10–20 minutes (a cast-iron dish or heavy cookbooks work nicely). Slice the tofu into thin strips ⅛–¼ inch (3–5mm) wide—the thinner the strips, the crispier the bacon! Then slice the strips again into small pieces about ¾ inch (2cm) long.
2. In a small bowl, combine the soy sauce, maple syrup and smoked paprika to make the marinade. Spread the tofu pieces over a large baking dish in a single layer, then pour over the marinade and soak for 10 minutes. The longer you leave it, the more flavor the tofu will absorb.
3. To cook in an air fryer, add the tofu bacon bits at 400°F (200°C) for 18 minutes, shaking halfway through. To cook in the oven, preheat to 400°F (210°C), place the tofu bits on a lined baking sheet and bake for 20–25 minutes, flipping halfway through; they are done when golden and slightly crispy. To pan-fry, heat about 2 tablespoons of vegetable oil in a skillet over medium-high and fry the tofu for 2–3 minutes on each side until golden, then rest on paper towel to absorb excess oil before serving—the tofu will get crispier after cooling.
4. To make the carbonara sauce, put the cashews in a small bowl and cover with boiling water for 10 minutes, then drain. Put the soaked cashews in a blender with the milk, lemon juice, garlic, nutritional yeast and miso paste and blitz until smooth. Taste and season with salt and pepper. Add extra water if you'd like a thinner consistency.
5. To serve, pour the sauce over hot pasta and mix in gently. Serve in bowls and top with the tofu bacon bits.

Great flavors—mild and good for every palate. We loved it. – Karissa

Before I went vegan, I used to love the idea of rich, creamy pasta sauces like alfredo. But whenever I'd order them at a restaurant, I couldn't finish the meal. As much as I enjoyed them at the start, they just quickly became a bit too rich. This cauliflower-based sauce still tastes decadent but without the heaviness.. A great way to sneak some hidden vegetables into your creamy pasta.

Cauliflower Alfredo

TOTAL TIME: 40 MINUTES
SERVES 4

1 medium head of cauliflower (about 1¾ pounds/800g), broken into florets
6 garlic cloves, unpeeled
4 tbsp olive oil
1 tsp vegetable bouillon powder
½ cup raw cashews
1 cup unsweetened plant-based milk
juice of ½ lemon
½ cup nutritional yeast
1 pound (500g) fettucine (cooked to package instructions) to serve
Seed or Nut Parmesan (page 12) to serve

1. Preheat the oven to 400°F (200°C).
2. Place the cauliflower florets and unpeeled garlic cloves on a baking sheet and coat well with 2 tablespoons of olive oil and the bouillon powder. Roast in the oven for 25–30 minutes or until the cauliflower is very soft and can be easily pierced by a fork (otherwise it won't blend smoothly). Roast for an extra 5–10 minutes if needed to get this texture.
3. While they are roasting, bring a small saucepan of water to a boil and cook the cashews for 10 minutes, then drain and rinse under cold water. (If your blender is not high-powered, I'd recommend soaking the cashews overnight or boiling them for 25 minutes to make them extra soft so the sauce is as silky smooth as possible.)
4. Remove the baking sheet from the oven and, when cool enough to touch, carefully peel the garlic.
5. Put the cooled cauliflower, roasted garlic, cashews, milk, lemon juice, nutritional yeast and remaining 2 tablespoons of olive oil in a blender and blitz until smooth. Taste and season with salt and pepper as desired, then blitz again to mix, adding an extra splash of milk if you'd like a thinner consistency.
6. Prepare the fettucine then drain and return to the pot. Pour the sauce over and stir to combine. Serve in bowls and top with parmesan.

NOTE

Safety tip! Never blend hot ingredients in a closed bullet-style blender, as the heat cannot escape and they can explode. To blend hot food, use a handheld blender or a regular standing blender with an opening for steam to escape. If you only have a closed bullet blender, wait for the ingredients to cool completely before blending. To be safe, always check your appliance manufacturer's temperature guidelines.

This was my very picky, non-vegan boyfriend's first completely vegan meal and he loved it. – Alana

Not only is this creamy chickpea pasta easy, quick, and zesty, it's also budget-friendly. A perfect hearty weeknight dinner made from mostly pantry staples.

Speedy Chickpea and Lemon Pasta

TOTAL TIME: 25 MINUTES
SERVES 4

1 pound (500g) spaghetti or pasta of choice
¼ cup olive oil
1 (14-ounce/400g) can chickpeas, drained and rinsed
6 garlic cloves, crushed
2 tsp finely chopped rosemary
2 tbsp white miso paste
1 cup nutritional yeast
1½ cups unsweetened plant-based milk
juice of 1 lemon
lemon wedges to serve

1. Cook the pasta to package instructions, reserving ½ cup of pasta water before draining.
2. While the pasta is cooking, prepare the sauce. Put the olive oil in a large skillet over medium heat and fry the chickpeas for 5–7 minutes, shaking the pan occasionally until they start to brown a little. Reduce the heat to low and add the garlic and rosemary, stirring for 1–2 minutes. Add the miso paste and nutritional yeast, stirring until the chickpeas are coated. Add the milk and increase the heat to medium to bring the sauce to a simmer. Stir constantly for a couple of minutes until the sauce begins to thicken, then add the lemon juice and continue to simmer for a few minutes. Taste and season with salt and pepper if desired and add a splash of pasta water if you prefer a thinner sauce.
3. Add the cooked spaghetti to the pan and stir gently with tongs to combine. Serve in pasta bowls with a wedge of lemon.

If you love butternut squash then this is the winter pasta recipe for you. The sauce is light, creamy and silky smooth with a hint of sweet caramel notes from the roasted squash and garlic. The sweetness is balanced out by the combination of peppery olive oil, lemon and rich toasted cashews and pine nuts in the pesto.

Creamy Squash Pasta with Basil Pesto

TOTAL TIME: 1 HOUR 5 MINUTES
SERVES 4

½ cup raw cashews
1⅔ pounds (750g) butternut squash
4 garlic cloves, unpeeled
2 tbsp extra-virgin olive oil
1 tsp vegetable bouillon powder
1 cup unsweetened plant-based milk
juice of ½ lemon
⅓ cup nutritional yeast
1 pound (500g) rigatoni or pasta of choice (cooked to package instructions) to serve
Seed or Nut Parmesan (page 12, optional) to serve

BASIL PESTO
¼ cup raw cashews
¼ cup pine nuts
2 cups loosely packed basil leaves
2 garlic cloves, roughly chopped
½ cup olive oil
½ tsp salt
juice of 1 lemon

1. Preheat the oven to 400°F (200°C).
2. Put the cashews in a small bowl and pour over enough boiling water to cover. Set aside to soak.
3. Peel and cut the squash into about 1½-inch (3–4cm) chunks. Place the squash and garlic cloves on a baking sheet and coat with the olive oil and bouillon powder. Roast for 40 minutes until the squash is golden and soft.
4. While the squash and garlic are roasting, prepare the pesto. Put the ¼ cup of raw cashews in a large skillet over medium-low heat and toast for 2 minutes, shaking the pan or stirring every 10–20 seconds. Reduce the heat to low and add the pine nuts, continuing to toast for 2–4 minutes and shaking the pan or stirring frequently to avoid burning. Remove from the heat once the nuts have golden brown highlights and are fragrant. Blitz the toasted nuts with the remaining pesto ingredients in a food processor or blender until mostly smooth with some small chunks of cashews (about 30 seconds to 1 minute), stopping and scraping down the sides if needed. If the pesto is too thick, add another 1–2 tablespoons of olive oil to loosen. Set aside.
5. Drain and rinse the soaked cashews. Once cool enough to touch, peel the roasted garlic cloves. Put the roasted squash, garlic, soaked cashews, milk, lemon juice, and nutritional yeast in a blender and blitz for 1–2 minutes until the sauce is smooth, stopping to scrape down the sides if needed.
6. Pour the squash sauce over the cooked pasta and stir to combine. Serve into bowls topped with a dollop of basil pesto and Seed or Nut Parmesan (if using).

NOTES

Safety tip! Never blend hot ingredients in a closed bullet-style blender, as the heat cannot escape and they can explode. To blend hot food, use a handheld blender or a standing blender with an opening for steam to escape. If you only have a closed bullet blender, wait for the ingredients to cool completely before blending. To be safe, always check your appliance manufacturer's temperature guidelines.

It was very simple to make, and you definitely wouldn't have known it was vegan. I liked that the sauce was low-key healthy but felt very indulgent and creamy. – Georgia

Creamy, fresh and punchy, this spinach avocado pasta sauce is loaded with vibrant greens and healthy fats. I know some people might be skeptical because avocado can have a bit of a funny taste when heated, but this recipe avoids that entirely, as the sauce is completely raw and only lightly heated by the cooked pasta. Don't skip the semi-dried tomatoes to garnish—their tangy sweetness really cuts through the creaminess!

Creamy Avocado Pasta with Semi-Dried Tomatoes

TOTAL TIME: 20 MINUTES
SERVES 4

½ cup cashews
1 pound (500g) linguine or pasta of choice
1 avocado
2½ cups (80g) loosely packed baby spinach
2 garlic cloves, roughly chopped
½ cup loosely packed basil leaves
½ cup olive oil
juice of 1 lemon
1 cup unsweetened plant-based milk
1 tsp salt
¼ tsp cracked pepper
1 cup semi-dried tomatoes or plump oil-packed sun-dried tomatoes, roughly chopped, to serve
basil leaves to garnish
Nut or Seed Parmesan (page 12, optional) to garnish

1. If you have time, soak the cashews in water overnight. Otherwise, boil the cashews in a small saucepan of water for 10 minutes. After soaking or boiling, drain and rinse under cold water. (If you do not have a high-powered blender, soak the cashews overnight or boil them for 25 minutes to make them extra soft and to get the sauce as silky smooth as possible.)
2. Cook the pasta according to package instructions.
3. While the pasta is cooking, put the drained cashews, avocado flesh, baby spinach, garlic, basil leaves, olive oil, lemon juice, milk, salt and pepper in a blender and blitz for 1–2 minutes until smooth.
4. Once pasta is cooked, drain and return to the saucepan. Pour the sauce over the cooked pasta and stir to combine.
5. Serve into bowls and top with tomatoes, extra basil and Seed or Nut Parmesan (if using).

This creamy red pepper pasta is quick, packed with vitamin C and delicious! Tangy, silky, earthy, and you'd never know it's vegan.

Creamy Roasted Red Pepper Pasta

TOTAL TIME: 1 HOUR
SERVES 4

2 red bell peppers
1 yellow onion, quartered
4 garlic cloves, unpeeled
1 tbsp olive oil
½ cup raw cashews
¼ cup nutritional yeast
¾ cup unsweetened plant-based milk
1½ tbsp white miso paste
¼ cup firmly packed basil leaves
2 tbsp tomato paste
1 pound (500g) rigatoni to serve
basil leaves to garnish
red pepper flakes to garnish (optional)

1. Preheat the oven to 350°F (180°C). Place the whole bell peppers, quartered onions, and garlic cloves on a lined baking sheet. Coat with the olive oil and a generous pinch of salt and pepper. Roast for 30 minutes. The bell peppers should be lightly charred on the ends.
2. While the vegetables are roasting, boil the cashews in a small saucepan of water for 10 minutes, then drain and rinse under cold water. (If your blender is not high-powered, I'd recommend soaking the cashews overnight or boiling them for 25 minutes to make them extra soft and to get the sauce as silky smooth as possible.)
3. Once the veggies are done, wrap the bell peppers in separate sheets of aluminum foil and leave them to sweat for 10 minutes. Carefully peel the skins off the peppers and remove and discard the stem and seeds. Cut the flesh into large chunks. Remove the garlic skins.
4. Put the roasted pepper and garlic in a blender with the nutritional yeast, milk, miso paste, basil and tomato paste and blitz until smooth. Taste and season with salt and pepper if desired. Add an extra splash of milk if you prefer a thinner consistency.
5. Pour the sauce over the cooked pasta, stirring to combine. Garnish with extra basil leaves and red pepper flakes (if using).

NOTES

Safety tip! Never blend hot ingredients in a closed bullet-style blender, as the heat cannot escape and they can explode. To blend hot food, use a handheld blender or a standing blender with an opening for steam to escape. If you only have a closed bullet blender, wait for the ingredients to cool completely before blending. To be safe, always check your appliance manufacturer's temperature guidelines.

The sauce was absolutely delicious. Good sauce to pasta ratio—I often worry that there won't be enough sauce because no one wants stodgy pasta, but it was the perfect amount. Very easy to follow, and while the recipe time is 1 hour, it's only about 10 minutes of actual work, which I love! – Georgia

It was really creamy without using cream. Also made for great leftovers the next day! – Karolinka

Not your traditional gnocchi but a totally delicious labor of love that is earthy, nutty, savory, and sweet all at once. Made using creamy tofu ricotta, this rustic meal is a fun recipe to make on the weekend when you have time to enjoy the process. The good news is that most of the heavy lifting is done by the food processor, but you still get to enjoy the fun part of shaping the soft, light dough. It will develop body after boiling and pan-frying. The result is tender pumpkin pieces with slightly caramelized notes, bouncy gnocchi, crisp sage leaves, and crunchy walnuts.

Pumpkin Ricotta Gnocchi

TOTAL TIME: 2 HOURS
SERVES 6

2 pounds (900g) pumpkin, skin removed, diced into 1¼-inch (3cm) chunks
1 tbsp olive oil
½ tsp salt
1 cup tofu ricotta (page 166)
2 cups all-purpose flour
3 tbsp olive oil
20 sage leaves
¾ cup walnuts
¼ cup olive oil
½ tsp salt
Seed or Nut Parmesan, to serve (page 12)

1. Preheat the oven to 425°F (220°C) and line a large roasting pan with parchment paper.
2. Spread the pumpkin over the roasting pan in a single layer and coat with the olive oil and salt. Roast in the oven for 20 minutes, then flip and roast for an additional 15–20 minutes or until it is tender but not soggy and has golden edges and highlights. Set aside half the pumpkin.
3. Put the tofu ricotta and the remaining half of the roast pumpkin in a food processor and blitz on high, stopping occasionally to scrape down the sides until well combined. Add the flour and pulse two or three times until just combined.
4. Dust a work surface with flour and gently shape the dough into a loaf. The dough will be very light and sticky, so use plenty of flour as needed. Slice into eight pieces, then roll each piece into a thin sausage about ¾ inch (2cm) wide. Slice into ½-inch (1½cm) pieces to make the gnocchi. If you like, roll each piece of gnocchi on a fork to get the classic ridged effect. Normally this is done to help sauce cling to the gnocchi, but for this recipe it is purely aesthetic.
5. Bring a large saucepan of salted water to a boil. Add the gnocchi to the water and boil until they rise to the surface (about 1–2 minutes). Drain.
6. Heat the olive oil in a large skillet over medium heat, then add the sage leaves, leaving plenty of space between them. Pan-fry for 30 seconds or until crispy, then remove to a plate lined with paper towel to drain. Next add the walnuts and fry for 2–3 minutes, stirring regularly, until they begin to turn golden. Remove from the pan and place with the sage leaves. Next, gently fry the reserved pumpkin pieces for 1–2 minutes on all sides until golden highlights begin to appear. Remove from the pan and place in a large mixing bowl.
7. If needed, put an extra glug of olive oil in the pan before adding only half the gnocchi (to avoid overcrowding). Fry for 2–3 minutes, stirring occasionally, until slightly crispy with golden highlights. Transfer to the bowl with the pumpkin, then repeat with remaining gnocchi. Combine the pumpkin and gnocchi very gently and season with salt and pepper to taste.
8. Serve immediately into bowls and top with the sage, walnuts and Seed or Nut Parmesan (if using).

NOTES

This dough does not handle like typical gnocchi made with eggs and potato, as it is very light, soft and sticky. It doesn't look like it will hold together at first, but trust me, it does. Don't be tempted to knead it, as this will make it too tough; just use plenty of flour when handling it. Wash any excess dough off your hands partway through shaping if needed.

You can use the gnocchi in this recipe with any sauce you would like. It would be delicious with a simple tomato sauce, ragu (see Classic Beef Lasagna on page 106) or even a creamy sauce—try it with the sauces from the Creamy Roasted Red Pepper Pasta (see page 160) or Semi-dried Tomato Pasta (see page 168) recipes. Remember, if you choose to make the gnocchi by itself, it only requires half the pumpkin called for in the ingredients list, about 14 ounces (400g).

Looking for an easy meal when entertaining? These giant stuffed pasta shells are one of my go-tos, perfect with garlic bread and a leafy salad on the side. You will need jumbo pasta shells for this recipe (known as conchiglioni in Italian), typically found at independent supermarkets and grocers. If you are hosting, I highly recommend preparing this in advance. You can make the individual components up to three days beforehand and bake on the day for a no-fuss homemade meal.

Ricotta and Spinach Stuffed Shells

TOTAL TIME: 1 HOUR 20 MINUTES
SERVES 6

½ pound (250g) jumbo pasta shells (conchiglioni)
½ pound (250g) frozen spinach, thawed
1 tbsp olive oil
1 medium yellow onion, finely diced
3 garlic cloves, crushed
2 tsp dried basil
½ tbsp brown sugar
1 tbsp soy sauce
6 cups (1.4L) tomato passata
roughly chopped parsley leaves to serve
Seed or Nut Parmesan (page 12) to serve

TOFU RICOTTA
1 pound (450g) extra firm tofu
½ cup almond meal
1 tbsp hemp seeds
juice of 1 lemon
2 tbsp olive oil
2 garlic cloves
2 tsp dried basil
1½ tsp salt
¼ cup nutritional yeast
pinch of ground black pepper

1. For the tofu ricotta, first press the tofu by placing the block between sheets of paper towel or wrapping in a clean, non-fluffy tea towel and weighing it down with a cutting board and some heavy objects for 30 minutes (a cast-iron dish or pan works nicely). Crumble the pressed tofu into a food processor and add the remaining ingredients, then blitz on high for 1 minute or until well combined, stopping occasionally to scrape down the sides if needed. The finished result should have a thick, creamy, ricotta-like consistency. Some small lumps are okay.
2. Preheat oven to 400°F (200°C) and cook the jumbo pasta shells according to package instructions.
3. While the pasta is cooking, squeeze the frozen spinach to remove as much liquid as possible, then pat dry and chop roughly. Mix with the tofu ricotta until well combined. Fill the cooked and drained pasta shells with the ricotta-spinach mixture.
4. Heat the olive oil in a large skillet over medium heat and sauté the onions for 2–3 minutes until translucent. Add the garlic and dried basil and stir for another minute. Add the brown sugar, soy sauce, and passata and stir to combine. Bring to a simmer, then reduce heat to low. Continue to simmer gently for 20–25 minutes, stirring occasionally, until the sauce has a rich tomato flavor and has thickened slightly.
5. Spread the sauce over the base of a 13 × 9-inch (33 × 22cm) baking dish. Nestle the stuffed shells into the sauce but do not cover them with sauce, as we want the tops of the shells to remain visible and get just a little crispy. Bake in the oven for 20 minutes. Serve topped with chopped parsley and Seed or Nut Parmesan (if using).

Loved how it had lots of sauce, and the filling was really tasty. I've made other stuffed shells before, and these are yummier! Leftovers reheated well in the oven, there was still plenty of sauce and the shells didn't dry out. – Larni

We've been making tofu ricotta for a while, but this was a different method and it worked so well. It was easy to follow, the steps were clear and it wasn't overly complicated. A new cook could easily make this and impress family and friends with it. – Caroline

This creamy pasta with basil is rich, a little sweet, tangy, and summery.

Semi-Dried Tomato Pasta

TOTAL TIME: 20 MINUTES
SERVES 4

½ cup raw cashews
1 pound (500g) pasta of choice
2 tbsp oil from the semi-dried tomatoes (or olive oil)
3 garlic cloves, crushed
¼ cup basil leaves
1¾ cups (200g) semi-dried tomatoes in oil, drained and roughly chopped
2 tbsp all-purpose flour
2 tbsp tomato paste
1 cup unsweetened plant-based milk
¾ cup vegetable stock
roughly chopped basil leaves to serve
Seed or Nut Parmesan (page 12) to serve

1. Boil the cashews in a small saucepan of water for 10 minutes, then drain and rinse under cold water. If your blender is not high-powered, I recommend soaking the cashews overnight or boiling them for 25 minutes to make them extra soft and to get the sauce as silky smooth as possible.
2. Cook the pasta according to package instructions.
3. While the pasta is cooking, heat the oil in a large saucepan over medium heat and sauté the garlic for 1 minute, then stir in fresh basil and about three-quarters of the semi-dried tomatoes. Add the flour, soaked cashews and tomato paste, stirring until the mixture is well combined. Gradually add the milk and vegetable stock, then simmer for 2 minutes until slightly thickened.
4. Transfer the sauce to a blender and blitz until smooth. Taste and season with salt and pepper as required, then blitz again. Add an extra splash of milk or water if the sauce is too thick.
5. Pour the sauce over the cooked pasta. Garnish with the remaining semi-dried tomatoes, basil leaves and Seed or Nut Parmesan.

NOTES

Safety tip! Never blend hot ingredients in a closed bullet-style blender, as the heat cannot escape and they can explode. To blend hot food, use a handheld blender or a standing blender with an opening for steam to escape. If you only have a closed bullet blender, wait for the ingredients to cool completely before blending. To be safe, always check your appliance manufacturer's temperature guidelines.

This is an ultra-creamy but wholesome plant-based twist on a classic American comfort food. Spinach and broccoli add color, bite, and extra goodness to this delicious pasta bake, which is topped with an addictive cheese-flavored crispy panko crumb topping. This recipe takes a bit of time but is definitely worth the effort.

Supergreen Mac 'n' Cheese Bake with Crispy Topping

TOTAL TIME: 1 HOUR 20 MINUTES
SERVES 6

2 cups raw cashews
1 pound (450g) macaroni
1 medium head of broccoli
¼ cup vegan margarine
1 leek, sliced
10 garlic cloves, chopped
5 cups (150g) loosely packed baby spinach
1 tsp onion powder or granulated onion
1 tsp smoked paprika
¼ cup all-purpose flour
½ cup nutritional yeast
½ tsp salt
½ tsp pepper
1 cup vegetable stock
2½ cups soy milk
4 tbsp white miso paste
1 tbsp apple cider vinegar

TOPPING

1 cup panko breadcrumbs
3 ounces (80g) vegan cheese, grated
3 tbsp hemp seeds
¼ cup olive oil
¼ cup nutritional yeast
1 tsp salt

1. Place the cashews in a small bowl and cover with boiling water. Soak for 10 minutes and drain.
2. Cook the macaroni according to the package instructions, reserving about ¼ cup of pasta water before draining.
3. Break the broccoli into small florets and cut the broccoli stem into ¾-inch (2cm) cubes.
4. While the pasta is cooking, melt the margarine in a large saucepan over medium heat and fry the leek for 2 minutes until softened and fragrant. Add the broccoli stalks and garlic and continue to cook for another 2 minutes. Add the cashews and baby spinach, stirring until the spinach has wilted. Add the onion powder or granulated onion, paprika, flour, nutritional yeast, salt and pepper and stir until well coated. Gradually add the stock and milk, stirring constantly. Stir in the miso paste and apple cider vinegar, then simmer for 5–10 minutes until the mixture has thickened.
5. Meanwhile, bring a medium pot of salted water to a rolling boil over high heat. Add the broccoli florets and boil for 3–4 minutes until tender but firm.
6. When the sauce has thickened, remove from the heat and transfer to a blender. Blitz until smooth, pausing to scrape down the sides if needed. This is the finished consistency of the sauce, so if it is too thick, add a splash of reserved pasta water or soy milk to loosen.
7. Return the sauce to the saucepan it was cooked in. Add the drained macaroni and broccoli florets and mix to combine. Transfer to a large 4-quart (3.3L) baking dish (about 13 × 9 inches/32 × 24cm) and smooth the top with the back of a spoon. Preheat the broiler to high.
8. Combine the topping ingredients in a bowl and mix well. Sprinkle over the pasta, then place the baking dish on the top rack of the oven and broil for 5–10 minutes or until golden. Keep a close eye on it to ensure it doesn't burn. Serve immediately.

NOTES

Leftovers will keep for up to five days in an airtight container in the refrigerator. The sauce will get much thicker after cooling and reheating but will still taste delicious!

Safety tip! Never blend hot ingredients in a closed bullet-style blender, as the heat cannot escape, and they can explode. To blend hot food, use a handheld blender or a standing blender with an opening for steam to escape. If you only have a closed bullet blender, wait for the ingredients to cool completely before blending. To be safe, always check your appliance manufacturer's temperature guidelines.

Salads

When I first described this recipe to my sister as one of my proudest creations for this cookbook, she gave me a suspicious glance and said, "That sounds nice, but is it really a salad?" We still haven't settled it, but my argument is that if it's served cold and has lots of vegetables, it's a salad.

Either way, this beauty is a spicy fusion of Mexican and Southern flavors, with charred corn, scallion, cilantro and avocado crema for an extra kick. The black beans and quinoa for protein make it a filling lunch, but it's also a deliciously fresh side dish.

Spicy Buffalo Cauliflower Salad with Zingy Avocado Crema

TOTAL TIME: 1 HOUR
SERVES 6

1 medium head of cauliflower (about 1¾ pounds/800g)
1 cup all-purpose flour
1½ cups unsweetened plant-based milk
2 tsp garlic powder
2 tsp onion powder
2 tsp smoked paprika
1 tsp salt
½ tsp black pepper
1½ cups panko breadcrumbs
2 tbsp cup sriracha hot sauce
2 tbsp soy sauce
3 tbsp vegetable oil
1 cup white quinoa
2 cups water
1 tsp vegetable bouillon powder
1 cup frozen corn kernels
1 (14-ounce/400g) can black beans, drained and rinsed
5 scallions, finely sliced
cilantro leaves for garnish

AVOCADO CREMA

⅓ cup raw cashews
1 avocado, pitted and peeled
½ cup loosely packed cilantro leaves
3 tbsp pickled jalapeño brine (or substitute water)
3–6 tbsp water
juice of 1 lime
1 garlic clove, roughly chopped
¼ tsp salt
3 pickled jalapeño slices, roughly chopped (optional)

1. For the avocado crema, boil the cashews in a small pot of water for 15 minutes to soften. Drain and rinse in cold water. Blitz the cashews and the remaining sauce ingredients on high in a blender until completely smooth, about 3 minutes. (Start with 3 tablespoons of the water and add more as required if the crema is too thick.) Stop to scrape down the sides if needed and add the extra water to loosen if necessary.
2. Lightly grease an air fryer basket with cooking spray or a small amount of oil or preheat oven to 425°F (220°C).
3. Break the cauliflower into bite-sized florets and remove any tough stems.
4. Whisk together the flour, milk, garlic powder, onion powder, paprika, salt and pepper in a large bowl until it forms a smooth batter.
5. Place the panko breadcrumbs in a separate mixing bowl.
6. Add the cauliflower pieces to the batter and mix with your hands until each floret is thoroughly coated. Next, roll the florets in the panko breadcrumbs, pressing gently to help them adhere. Air-fry the cauliflower at 400°F (200°C) for 15 minutes or bake in the oven for 20-25 minutes, flipping halfway through.
7. While the cauliflower is cooking, prepare the buffalo sauce by combining the sriracha, soy sauce, and vegetable oil in a small bowl.
8. Transfer the cooked cauliflower to a large mixing bowl. Pour the buffalo sauce over and toss gently until thoroughly coated. Return the cauliflower to the air fryer or oven for another 10–15 minutes.
9. Put the quinoa, water, and bouillon powder in a medium pot and bring to a boil, then cover and reduce the heat to low. Simmer for 15 minutes, then remove from heat. Leave covered for 10 minutes, then fluff with a fork.
10. While the quinoa is cooking, put the frozen corn kernels in a small skillet over medium-high heat and leave them to char (do not stir). After 3–5 minutes, check a couple of kernels to see if they have little black highlights, then shake the pan for 1–3 minutes until they are evenly charred. Remove from heat.
11. Tip the cooked quinoa into a large mixing bowl. Add the drained black beans, charred corn, and scallion and toss to combine. Spoon into individual bowls or a large salad dish. Top with the buffalo cauliflower and add dollops of avocado crema. Garnish with cilantro leaves and serve immediately.

NOTES

In a hurry? Speed up this recipe by swapping the Avocado Crema for a diced avocado.

Loved the zingy flavors. Crema was amazing. – Sue

This pasta salad was inspired by a BLT sandwich, minus the lettuce! It's creamy, fresh and punchy, with lots of contrasting crunchy and silky textures. The tempeh bacon turns crispy on the edges and a little chewy, almost like a vegan jerky! Perfect as a substantial side dish for a summer barbecue.

Creamy Avocado Pasta Salad with Tempeh Bacon

TOTAL TIME: 40 MINUTES
SERVES 6

12 ounces (350g) bowtie pasta (or pasta shape of choice)
3 tsp olive oil
11 ounces (300g) tempeh
¼ cup soy sauce
2 tbsp maple syrup
2½ tsp smoked paprika
2 (14-ounce/400g) cans chickpeas, drained and rinsed
½ tbsp extra-virgin olive oil
1 tsp salt
1 tsp ground cumin
1 tsp ground turmeric
1½ cups (250g) cherry tomatoes, halved
½ red onion, finely sliced
⅓ cup loosely packed dill, finely chopped

AVOCADO DRESSING

1 large avocado, pitted and peeled
2½ cups (80g) loosely packed baby spinach
⅓ cup loosely packed dill
¼ cup plant-based unsweetened natural yogurt
¼ cup plant-based mayonnaise, store bought or homemade (page 208)
juice of 1 lemon
1 garlic clove
½ tsp onion powder
1 tsp salt
¼ tsp cracked black pepper

1. Cook the pasta according to package instructions, then drain and rinse under cold water. Drizzle 1 teaspoon of the olive oil over the pasta and gently mix to minimize sticking. Set aside and allow pasta to cool completely.
2. Preheat the oven to 400°F (200°C) or prepare an air fryer.
3. Slice the block of tempeh in half lengthways, then into thin strips approximately ¼ inch (½cm) wide. Combine the soy sauce, maple syrup, 2 teaspoons of olive oil, and 2 teaspoons of paprika in a medium bowl to make a marinade. Taste and adjust flavor as needed; it should be salty, smoky, and sweet (the sweetness may seem excessive, but it's needed to balance the inherent bitterness of the tempeh). Add the tempeh to the marinade bowl and massage with your hands. Leave to soak for 10–15 minutes.
4. Combine the chickpeas with the extra-virgin olive oil, salt, ground cumin, ground turmeric, and remaining ½ teaspoon of paprika in a bowl and mix well.
5. Air fryer method: add the tempeh bacon to one half of the basket and the chickpeas to the other. Air-fry for 15–20 minutes at 400°F (200°C), shaking halfway through so they crisp evenly.
6. Oven method: transfer the tempeh pieces with tongs onto a lined baking sheet in a single layer. Set aside the marinade. Place the chickpeas on another lined baking sheet in a single layer. Bake the tempeh for 15 minutes, then remove from the oven, flip, and brush generously with the reserved marinade. Bake for another 10 minutes until browned and edges are lightly charred. Bake the chickpeas for 15 minutes, then shake the pan so they cook evenly and return to the oven for another 10–15 minutes or until they are golden brown and crispy.
7. For the avocado dressing, blitz all the ingredients in a blender until smooth, stopping and scraping down the sides if needed.
8. To serve, place the pasta and avocado dressing in a very large bowl and mix until coated. Gently toss in the cherry tomatoes, red onion, and dill, then top with the chickpeas and tempeh bacon.

The dressing was phenomenal, and I will always make tempeh this way moving forward! Very satisfying meal all around. Tempeh has always been a bit too bitter for me, and this marinade made it absolutely perfect. I have also struggled with how much to season crispy chickpeas in the past, and this was spot-on!
– Cybelle

Say hello to your new favorite lunch! This filling and mildly spiced roast cauliflower salad is so satisfying. It's the ultimate texture party, with bouncy pearl couscous, crisp almonds, fresh onion, and chewy dried cranberries. Topped with my go-to Creamy Dreamy Lime Tahini Dressing (see page 200), it mixes sweet, spicy, and tangy flavors.

I grew up knowing cauliflower only in its boiled form, and unsurprisingly, I wasn't a fan. It wasn't until I tried roasted cauliflower that I finally got it. Something magical happens in the oven, and those little florets transform from bland and crumbly to slightly nutty, sweet, and buttery.

It tastes best fresh (naturally), but as far as salads go, this one holds up pretty well in the fridge too.

Curried Cauliflower Salad with Pearl Couscous

TOTAL TIME: 40 MINUTES
SERVES 6

- 1 large head of cauliflower (about 2 pounds/900g), broken into bite-size florets
- 3 tbsp extra-virgin olive oil
- 2 tsp curry powder
- ½ tsp ground cumin
- ½ tsp garlic powder
- ½ tsp ground turmeric
- ¼ tsp dried chili powder, optional
- ½ tsp salt
- 1 cup pearl couscous
- 1 tsp vegetable bouillon powder
- ½ red onion, thinly sliced
- 1 (14-ounce/400g) can lentils, drained and rinsed
- ¼ cup dried cranberries or currants
- ½ cup firmly packed parsley leaves, roughly chopped
- Creamy Dreamy Lime Tahini Dressing (page 200)
- ½ cup roughly chopped almonds, toasted, to garnish

1. Preheat the oven to 400°F (200°C).
2. In a large mixing bowl, combine the cauliflower florets, 2 tablespoons of the olive oil, curry powder, ground cumin, garlic powder, ground turmeric, chili powder (if using), and salt. Toss well to coat.
3. Spread the cauliflower over a baking sheet lined with parchment paper and drizzle with the remaining tablespoon of olive oil. Roast in the oven for 25–30 minutes or until the cauliflower is tender, stirring the mixture halfway through for even browning. Set aside to cool.
4. Cook the pearl couscous according to package instructions but add the bouillon powder in place of any salt. Once cooked, fluff the couscous with a fork and set aside to cool.
5. Combine the cooled pearl couscous, roasted cauliflower, red onion, lentils, dried cranberries, and parsley in a large salad bowl. Pour the Creamy Dreamy Lime Tahini Dressing over and toss gently to coat all the ingredients. Garnish with toasted almonds and serve.

NOTES

Need a gluten-free option? Substitute pearl couscous with quinoa.

Don't have parsley? Try fresh cilantro leaves instead.

It had everything! It was light but hearty; sweet and savory; fresh and caramelized. Just perfection. Exactly the kind of meal I could see making weekly because it is so easy, and many of these ingredients are already in the pantry. – Cybelle

This refreshing summer salad is tangy, spicy, and sweet, the perfect way to use some nectarines during stone fruit season. This would also be delicious with peaches.

Nectarine Salad

TOTAL TIME: 15 MINUTES
SERVES 4

10 nectarines, pitted and sliced into 8 pieces
3 Persian (mini) cucumbers, sliced into matchsticks
¼ cup mint leaves, torn
½ cup raw cashews, toasted

DRESSING

juice of 1 lemon
3 tbsp mirin
¼ tsp salt
2 tbsp olive oil
1 fresh red chili, finely sliced (optional)

1. Combine the dressing ingredients in a jar and shake to combine.
2. Place the nectarines, cucumbers, mint, and cashews in a large bowl, pour the dressing over the top and toss to coat. Transfer to a serving bowl and serve immediately.

In a nutshell, this is a bitter, fresh, sweet, and anise-scented salad that looks beautiful and is full of contrasting flavors. If you haven't tried it before, radicchio is very bitter and quite polarizing—you either love it or hate it. I am obviously in the former camp. I first tried it years ago alongside a cheese pizza at a Melbourne restaurant. I was kind of shocked when I took my first bite, as I was expecting it to taste light and a little grassy, like regular red lettuce. But when paired with a rich meal like pizza or pasta, radicchio really shines, and this classic combination of sweet orange and fennel balance out the bitterness. I suggest serving it with a creamy or cheesy dish for contrast—try it with my Ricotta and Spinach Stuffed Shells (see page 166), Classic Beef Lasagna (see page 106), or Creamy Roasted Red Pepper Pasta (see page 160).

Radicchio, Orange, and Fennel Salad

TOTAL TIME: 30 MINUTES
SERVES 4

1 small head of radicchio
2 navel oranges
1 fennel bulb
3 tbsp olive oil

1. Fill a large mixing bowl with cold water and ice. Remove any damaged outer leaves from the radicchio. Slice it in half and carefully remove and discard the core without slicing all the way through. Separate the leaves and place in the ice water, leaving to soak for 15 minutes; this will help reduce some of the bitterness.
2. Place a colander over a medium mixing bowl. Trim the ends of the oranges, then slice off the skin on all sides. Slice the oranges into rounds, placing each into the colander as you go. Set aside for the drips to catch in the bowl.
3. Trim the ends of the fennel, reserving the fronds. Halve the bulb, remove and discard the core, then slice very thinly.
4. Make the dressing by mixing the olive oil with the caught orange juice drips and season with salt and cracked black pepper.
5. Place the radicchio leaves on a clean tea towel to dry. Once dried, arrange them on a large serving platter in a single layer, with leaves overlapping. Place the orange rounds and fennel slices on top of the radicchio.
6. When you're ready to serve, pour the salad dressing over the top and garnish with a few reserved fennel fronds.

This hearty salad is nourishing, balanced, seasoned with Middle Eastern-inspired spices and fresh herbs, and has my favorite Creamy Dreamy Lime Tahini Dressing (see page 200). It's a healthy craveable lunch or dense side dish. If you have one, use an air fryer to cook the chickpeas and make them extra crispy.

Roasted Cauliflower Salad with Tahini, Chickpeas, and Pearl Couscous

TOTAL TIME: 45 MINUTES
SERVES 4

1½ tsp ground cumin
1½ tsp ground coriander
1 tsp smoked paprika
1 tsp salt
½ tsp ground turmeric
¼ tsp dried chili powder
1 medium head of cauliflower (about 1¾ pounds/800g), broken into florets
3 tbsp olive oil
1 (14-ounce/400g) can chickpeas, drained and rinsed
1 cup pearl couscous
2 cups water
1 tsp vegetable bouillon powder
½ red onion, thinly sliced
½ cup parsley, roughly chopped
½ cup mint, roughly chopped
Creamy Dreamy Lime Tahini Dressing (page 200)

1. Preheat the oven to 425°F (220°C).
2. In a small bowl, combine the ground cumin, ground coriander, smoked paprika, salt, ground turmeric, and chili powder.
3. Place the cauliflower florets in a large mixing bowl, drizzle with half the olive oil and about three-quarters of the spice mix and use your hands to coat the florets thoroughly. Transfer to a large baking sheet lined with parchment paper in a single layer. Drizzle with an extra tablespoon of olive oil and roast in the oven for 25–30 minutes or until the cauliflower is golden and tender when pierced with a fork.
4. Add the chickpeas to the same bowl used for the cauliflower and coat with the remaining olive oil and spice mix. Toss or stir to coat.
5. Air fryer option (recommended): tip the chickpeas into the basket and cook for 15 minutes at 400°F (200°C), shaking halfway through. The chickpeas should be golden and crispy.
6. Oven option: transfer the chickpeas to a second baking sheet lined with parchment paper. Roast for 30 minutes or until golden and slightly crispy.
7. While the chickpeas and cauliflower are roasting, prepare the pearl couscous. In a medium saucepan, bring the water and bouillon powder to a boil. Add the pearl couscous and cook for as long as indicated on the package instructions. Once cooked, fluff the couscous with a fork and set aside to cool.
8. In a large salad bowl, combine the cooked pearl couscous, roasted cauliflower and chickpeas, finely chopped red onion, parsley, and mint. Pour over the Creamy Dreamy Lime Tahini Dressing and toss gently to coat all the ingredients. Serve and enjoy!

NOTE

I highly recommend using an air fryer to get your chickpeas ultra-crispy! The oven will also work to make them golden and firm, but they won't achieve the same level of crunch.

This dense and filling grain salad is delicious with bouncy, chewy freekeh and roasted eggplant. The recipe calls for fresh parsley, but any soft herbs like cilantro, dill, or mint will taste lovely, so feel free to experiment and use up what you have in the fridge.

Roasted Eggplant and Grain Salad with Tahini

TOTAL TIME: 1 HOUR
SERVES 4

1 cup freekeh
½ tsp vegetable bouillon powder
3 cups water
2 large eggplants (about 2½ pounds/1kg), ends trimmed and cut into 1¼-inch (3cm) cubes
2 tbsp olive oil
½ tsp salt
1 (14-ounce/400g) can lentils, drained and rinsed
1 red onion, finely diced
⅓ cup slivered almonds, toasted
1 cup flat-leaf parsley, roughly chopped
tahini to serve
lemon wedges to serve

DRESSING

juice of 1 lemon
2 garlic cloves, crushed
½ tsp salt
¼ tsp cracked pepper
1 tbsp pomegranate molasses or red wine vinegar
1 tbsp olive oil
1 tsp agave or maple syrup

1. Preheat the oven to 425°F (220°C).
2. Place the freekeh, vegetable bouillon, and water in a medium saucepan and bring to a boil over high heat, then reduce to the lowest heat possible. Cover and cook for the time indicated on the package instructions or until tender and liquid is absorbed. (I normally cook freekeh for 40 minutes, but this will vary.) Set aside to cool to room temperature.
3. Coat the eggplant pieces in olive oil and salt, then spread over a large baking sheet in a single layer and roast for 15 minutes. Flip the eggplant pieces and return to oven for another 20 minutes or until tender with some golden highlights.
4. To make the dressing, add all the ingredients to a jar, seal, and shake well.
5. Put the freekeh, roasted eggplant, lentils, red onion, almonds, and parsley in a salad bowl. Pour the dressing over the top and toss to coat. Serve with a generous drizzle of tahini and lemon wedges.

NOTES

Really good tahini is typically quite runny, but supermarket varieties can often be stiff and thick (especially if you are reaching the bottom of your jar). If your tahini is too thick to drizzle over the salad, loosen it by mixing with a splash of mild olive oil or warm water.

Sauce

Condi

s and

ments

An essential roast dinner accompaniment, you'd never know this rich brown gravy is actually vegan. Made with mostly pantry items in a flash.

10-Minute Gravy

TOTAL TIME: 10 MINUTES
MAKES 1 MEDIUM JUG

2 rosemary sprigs
4 thyme sprigs
1 cup vegetable stock
1 cup water
2 tsp balsamic vinegar
2 tbsp soy sauce
3 tbsp plant-based butter or margarine
¼ cup all-purpose flour
½ tsp onion powder
½ tsp garlic powder

1. Tie the sprigs of rosemary and thyme together with cooking twine.
2. Combine the stock, water, balsamic vinegar and soy sauce in a liquid measuring cup.
3. Melt the butter or margarine in a medium saucepan over low heat, then whisk in the flour, onion powder, and garlic powder for 1–2 minutes until it forms a thick paste. Gradually pour the stock mixture into the flour paste, whisking constantly to avoid lumps forming. Once you have added all the liquid, place the tied herb sprigs in the pot, increase the heat to medium, and bring to a simmer, stirring occasionally, until the gravy thickens, about 3–5 minutes.
4. Remove the herbs and season with salt and pepper to taste. Serve immediately over roast vegetables, hot fries, or however you like to enjoy your gravy! Leftover gravy can be stored in the refrigerator for up to five days.

Even if you're not vegan, this is a very sweet, light, and, frankly, just gorgeous apple syrup. Perfect on toast, as a sweetener in tea or in any dish you'd normally use honey.

Apple Honey

TOTAL TIME: 30 MINUTES
MAKES 1 SMALL JAR

3 cups apple juice
¾ cup sugar
juice of ½ lemon

1. Place all the ingredients in a small saucepan over medium heat and stir to combine. Dip a wooden skewer into the mixture and mark the depth of the liquid on it with a marker. When the honey begins to boil, reduce the heat to low and simmer for about 20–30 minutes until reduced by half (check by dipping the skewer back into the liquid and comparing it to the original marked depth). The honey will still look very thin and watery while hot, but as long as it has reduced and is a slightly darker golden, it's done—don't wait until it looks thicker or it will harden to apple toffee.
2. Allow the honey to cool slightly, then transfer to a glass jar while still warm. It will thicken as it cools. Keep it in the pantry for up to two weeks or in the refrigerator for a month.

NOTES

This is a very simple recipe, but it can go wrong quite easily if you overcook your honey, as it will turn into toffee. I am speaking from experience! As mentioned in the recipe, do not be tempted to wait until the honey is noticeably thicker—it should still be watery and runny. Use a small saucepan so you can easily see the difference in the height on your skewer.

If stored in the refrigerator, the consistency will be much firmer than if left at room temperature in the pantry. If your honey turned out runnier than you would like it to be, storing it in the refrigerator can be a way to compensate.

WECK

This is my favorite fresh and zingy sauce to dollop onto salads, tacos, and sandwiches. You will see it called for in multiple recipes throughout this book—it's surprisingly versatile. Use it to take your meal to the next level with healthy fats, acid, and a little spice.

Zingy Avocado Crema

TOTAL TIME: 20 MINUTES
MAKES ABOUT 1 CUP

⅓ cup raw cashews (or substitute sunflower seeds)
1 avocado, pitted and peeled
½ cup loosely packed cilantro leaves
3 tbsp pickled jalapeño brine (or substitute water)
3–6 tbsp water
juice of 1 lime (approx. 2 tbsp)
1 garlic clove, roughly chopped
¼ tsp salt
1 tbsp pickled jalapeño slices (optional)

1. Bring a small saucepan of water to a boil and simmer the cashews for 15 minutes to soften. Drain and rinse in cold water.
2. Put the cashews in a blender with the remaining ingredients. Start by adding only 3 tablespoons of the water and blending on high until completely smooth, about 3 minutes. Stop to scrape down the sides if needed and add the extra water to loosen if the crema is too thick.

This is one of those versatile recipes I keep in my back pocket and use over and over again—it packs so much flavor, is simple to prepare, and tastes just as delicious as any conventional parmesan-based pesto. If you're looking for ways to use it, check out my Pesto Cannellini Beans (see page 134), Roasted Vegetable Sandwich with Pesto (see page 94), Tomato Tarts with Basil Pesto (see page 88), or Hearty Yellow Split Pea Soup with Basil Pesto (see page 102).

Basil Pesto

TOTAL TIME: 15 MINUTES
MAKES 1 SMALL JAR

¼ cup raw cashews
3 tbsp pine nuts
2 cups loosely packed basil leaves
2 garlic cloves, roughly chopped
½ cup olive oil
½ tsp salt
juice of 1 lemon

1. Toast the cashews in a large, dry skillet over medium-low heat for 2 minutes, shaking the pan or stirring every 20 seconds or so. Reduce the heat to low, then add the pine nuts and continue to toast for 2–4 minutes, shaking the pan frequently to avoid burning. Remove from the heat once the nuts have golden brown highlights and are fragrant.
2. Add the cashews, pine nuts, and remaining ingredients to a food processor or blender and blitz until mostly smooth with some small chunks of cashews remaining (about 30 seconds to 1 minute), stopping to scrape down the sides as needed. If the pesto is too thick, add an extra 1–2 tablespoons of olive oil to loosen.

This is a deliciously sweet and spicy addition to any savory meal. Whenever I make a batch, it doesn't last long. I'll eat it on everything—sandwiches, nachos, avocado toast, tofu scramble, with sour cream (like a sweet-chili dip), or even just on bread by itself. It requires minimal hands-on time and only a few ingredients. Remember that your chili jam will be as hot as the chilies you use! I've tried this with regular cayenne chilies and small bird's-eye chilies. I much prefer the cayenne, as I have a pretty low heat tolerance, but if you want something more fiery, use a hotter variety. Pro tip: wear gloves so you don't accidentally rub chili into your eyes!

Chili Jam

TOTAL TIME: 45 MINUTES
MAKES 2 GENEROUS CUPS (500ML)

15 fresh red chilies (any variety, I prefer cayenne)
2 red bell peppers
8 garlic cloves, roughly chopped
3 cups sugar
3 cups (750ml) apple cider vinegar

1. Roughly chop the chilies and bell peppers, discarding the stems and seeds. Put the chilies in a food processor with the garlic and blitz until finely chopped. Add the bell pepper and pulse again until finely chopped.
2. Put the chili, garlic, and bell pepper mixture in a large saucepan over medium-high heat along with the sugar and vinegar. Bring to a boil, then reduce to a simmer over low heat for 40 minutes. Stir occasionally until the liquid has reduced by roughly half. The consistency will be thicker but still runny.
3. Pour into sterilized jars and seal while still hot. The jam will continue to set as it cools. Unopened, it will keep in the pantry for up to four months. Once opened, keep in the fridge for up to three weeks.

This is a zesty, creamy salad dressing that I go back to time and time again. You'll find it used with my Roasted Cauliflower Salad with Tahini, Chickpeas, and Pearl Couscous (see page 184). It's also very tasty drizzled over roast pumpkin, in wraps and sandwiches, stirred into soup, or as a dip with carrot sticks.

Creamy Dreamy Lime Tahini Dressing

TOTAL TIME: 5 MINUTES
SERVES 4

⅓ cup tahini
juice of 1 lime
3–5 tbsp water
1½ tsp garlic powder
½ tsp ground cumin

1. In a small bowl, whisk the tahini, lime juice, 3 tablespoons of the water, garlic powder, ground cumin, and a pinch of salt until well combined. Taste and adjust seasoning with extra salt and pepper if desired. If needed, adjust the consistency by adding more water.
2. Store in a jar in the refrigerator for up to three days, stirring before use if any separation occurs.

A well-loved accidentally vegan spread, made from spiced Belgian speculoos biscuits. My whole-food version is made using roasted cashews, almonds, and the same warming spices of cinnamon, ginger, clove, and nutmeg. It's still rich and decadent, but with more nutritional value.

Healthier "Speculoos" Spread

TOTAL TIME: 25 MINUTES
MAKES 1 SMALL JAR

1 cup raw cashews
1 cup raw almonds
2 tbsp maple syrup
1 tsp vanilla extract
1 tsp ground cinnamon
½ tsp ground ginger
¼ tsp ground cloves
¼ tsp ground nutmeg
2 tbsp canola or other neutral-flavored oil (optional)

1. Preheat the oven to 350°F (175°C). Spread the raw nuts evenly over a baking sheet and roast for 18–20 minutes until fragrant and lightly golden, rotating the tray halfway through so they are evenly golden. Keep an eye on them to avoid burning, as ovens vary.
2. Allow the roasted nuts to cool slightly before transferring them to a food processor or high-powered blender. Blitz on a high speed for a few minutes until they break down and start to become creamy, scraping down the sides occasionally if needed to ensure even blending. Add the maple syrup, vanilla extract, spices, and a pinch of salt and continue blending until well combined and the nut butter reaches the desired consistency. Add the canola oil and blitz again if you would prefer a runnier and smoother consistency. Taste and add more syrup or spices if desired.
3. Transfer to a glass jar and store in the refrigerator for two to three weeks. Before each use, let it sit at room temperature for a few minutes to soften, or use it exclusively on toast to help make it more spreadable.

Chia jam is a healthy, low-sugar breakfast spread loaded with omega-3s, plant protein, and fiber that's handy for any plant person to have up their sleeve. Use it as a topping on porridge, stirred through yogurt, on toast, or anywhere you might use jam.

Quick and Easy Chia Jam

TOTAL TIME: 12 MINUTES
MAKES 1 SMALL JAR

1 cup frozen berries of choice
1 tbsp water
agave or maple syrup or sugar to taste (optional)
1 tbsp chia seeds

1. Place the berries in a small saucepan with the water and stir constantly over medium heat until they have broken down (5–7 minutes). Taste and add the syrup or sugar if desired (I like to leave it tangy, without added sugar). Stir in the chia seeds and turn off the heat. Leave to cool, and the chia seeds will begin to soak up the liquid and thicken the mixture.
2. Transfer to a glass jar, seal, and refrigerate for a few hours to set more. Chia jam will keep in the fridge for one week.

This super-simple chili oil is a pantry essential in our house. I drizzle it on curries, tofu scramble, tacos, hummus—any savory dish that could use a little extra oomph. Many chili oils have a long list of ingredients, but this one is the simplest version of all: red pepper flakes and vegetable oil.

My husband, Steve, was first to get into making this. It was taught to us by a Chinese-Australian friend and housemate of Steve's from university. One of my core memories of our university years is walking through the door of their run-down shared house in Brunswick and nearly choking on the freshly made chili oil in the air. If it immediately hits the back of your throat and induces a coughing fit, you're doing it right! Jing was a true chili lover and made a batch almost every week. For us mere mortals, though, this jar will probably last a month or more.

Chili Oil

TOTAL TIME: 10 MINUTES
MAKES 1 JAR, ABOUT 1⅓ CUP (325ML)

⅓ cup red pepper flakes
pinch of salt
1½ cups vegetable oil (canola, sunflower or similar neutral oil)

1. Put the red pepper flakes and salt in a medium heatproof bowl.
2. Heat the oil in a small saucepan over medium heat until it reaches 230–250°F (110–120°C). The time it takes to reach this temperature will depend on your stove and the size of your pot, but generally it should be 3–6 minutes. If you don't have a thermometer, test by placing the tip of a wooden chopstick into the oil, and if there is some slight bubbling (it doesn't need to be a lot) then you're ready to go. If the oil is smoking, bubbling, or spitting, then it's too hot.
3. Pour the hot oil over the red pepper flakes—be careful, as it will bubble up. Allow to cool before sealing in a sterilized glass jar.

NOTES

You can pour the oil directly into a jar instead of a bowl only if it is large enough to accommodate the bubbling up *and* is made from thick heat-resistant glass. I used a Weck 19.6-ounce (580ml) sturz preserving jar and it was fine, but a regular glass jar would likely crack from the heat, so please choose carefully and do so at your own risk.

If preferred, you can strain out the red pepper flakes after cooling.

Chili oil will keep at room temperature in a cool, dark place like a pantry for about two months, sometimes longer. If the color changes, it smells sweet, rancid (fermented) or you see any signs of mold, throw it out. If you live in a hot climate, consider keeping it in the fridge; however, it will thicken and congeal, so you'll need to scoop a little out and bring it to room temperature when you want to use it.

Some vegan mayos taste sweet and tangy, but I can proudly say this tastes just like a whole egg mayonnaise—salty, fatty, smooth, and light. Plus, it's made from something you'd normally throw down the drain: aquafaba! That's the cloudy liquid from a can of chickpeas. Next time you open a can, save the aquafaba and make this recipe. It's affordable, rich, and quick.

Whole Egg–Style Mayonnaise

TOTAL TIME: 15 MINUTES
MAKES 1 JAR, ABOUT 1½ CUPS (350ML)

⅓ cup aquafaba
1 tbsp apple cider vinegar (or substitute lemon juice)
2 tsp Dijon mustard
½ tsp salt
1 cup vegetable or other neutral oil (e.g., sunflower, canola)

1. Blitz all the ingredients except the oil in a food processor or a blender for 10 seconds to combine. Turn to medium speed and slowly pour a very thin trickle of oil into the machine while it is running. It is critical that you pour the oil in *very* slowly and only while the machine is running, otherwise the mixture will split. The mixture will gradually turn white and creamy and thicken. Continue until all the oil is combined, then taste and add more salt if desired.
2. Transfer into a sterilized glass jar (see page 20) and keep in the fridge for up to two weeks.

Sweet

Treats

This nostalgic and no-fuss pudding takes 5 minutes to prep and requires minimal cleanup. You throw all the ingredients into the baking dish and it goes into the oven to do its thing. Remember to put it on before you start making dinner, and by the time you're done you'll have a cozy dessert to enjoy, perfect for winter. As the pudding bakes, a skin will form on top that you can eat or remove. Skin or no skin, I recommend serving this with extra oat milk and a sprinkle of cinnamon sugar. Snuggle up with it on the couch and enjoy.

Baked Rice Pudding

TOTAL TIME: 2 HOURS 10 MINUTES
SERVES 6

1 cup short- or medium-grain white rice, rinsed
⅓ cup sugar
½ tsp ground cinnamon
¼ tsp ground nutmeg
¼ tsp salt
4 cups oat milk
1 tsp vanilla extract
1 cup canned unsweetened coconut cream
cinnamon sugar to serve
oat milk to serve

1. Preheat the oven to 325°F (160°C). Lightly grease an 8-cup (2L) capacity ovenproof dish that is at least 2¾ inches (7cm) deep.
2. Put all the ingredients in the dish and carefully stir to combine.
3. Bake uncovered for 1 hour 45 minutes, then taste the rice—it should be very soft and sticky, but it's okay if there is a little bit of excess liquid on the bottom. If there is still a lot of milk remaining or the rice isn't super soft, continue to bake for an additional 10–15 minutes. The pudding will form a skin on top with brown highlights.
4. Serve in bowls and top with cinnamon sugar and oat milk.

NOTE

This recipe uses a lot of milk, but it is necessary for such a long bake time. The finished result will be a super-soft rice pudding that is a little runny (in a good way). Yum!

Quick and easy to assemble with pantry staples. The extra cinnamon and coconut cream made it really delicious. Best rice pudding I've ever had! – Kate

The ease! No stirring and being bound to the stove for over an hour just for your rice pudding to have a burnt bottom anyway or your milk to cook over. The texture is lovely, and I really enjoy the nutmeg! It adds a little citrusy note to a familiar flavor. Classic comfort food! – Kerstin

Call me basic, but I love energy balls. They're handy for a snack on the go and way tastier than any muesli bar. This combination of rich cacao, coconut, and tangy cranberries is so appealing. I love having a couple of these as a late-morning snack with coffee.

Cacao, Cranberry, and Oat Energy Balls

TOTAL TIME: 10 MINUTES + 30 MINUTES CHILLING TIME
MAKES 10

1 cup rolled oats or quick oats
½ cup dried cranberries
¼ cup cacao powder
¼ cup finely shredded coconut
⅛ tsp salt
¼ cup maple syrup or agave nectar
⅓ cup almond butter or any nut or seed butter of choice
1 tsp vanilla extract

1. In a large mixing bowl, combine the oats, dried cranberries, cacao powder, coconut, and salt.
2. In a separate small bowl, mix the maple syrup with the almond butter and vanilla extract.
3. Add the wet almond butter mixture to the dry ingredients and mix well. It will seem dry at first, but eventually it will become sticky and hold together when pressed.
4. Lightly wet your hands. Take about 1 tablespoon of the mixture and roll it into a ball with your hands. Repeat until all the mixture is used, making about ten balls in total.
5. Place the balls in an airtight container and chill in the refrigerator for 30 minutes to firm up. They will keep in the refrigerator for up to a week.

This chewy popcorn slice (bar) with dark chocolate is a tasty treat that's perfect for morning or afternoon tea. It's budget-friendly and makes a big batch.

Caramel Popcorn Slice

TOTAL TIME: 30 MINUTES
MAKES 16

¼ cup vegetable oil
½ cup popcorn kernels
5¼ ounces (150g) plant-based dark chocolate
sea salt flakes

CARAMEL

7 tbsp (3½ ounces/100g) plant-based butter or margarine
1 cup brown sugar
½ cup brown rice or golden syrup
1 tsp vanilla extract
½ tsp salt
½ tsp baking soda

1. Lightly grease a large baking dish about 14 × 10 inches (36 × 25cm).
2. Heat the oil in a large saucepan over medium heat. Add a few corn kernels and wait until they pop, then quickly remove. Add the remaining popcorn, lifting and shaking the saucepan to spread the kernels out evenly. Cover with a lid. Once the popcorn starts popping, shake gently once.
3. Remove from heat when the popping slows down and you can count to three between pops. Transfer the popcorn to a very large bowl and pick out any kernels that didn't pop.
4. To make the caramel, wipe the saucepan clean then melt the butter over low heat. Add the sugar, syrup, vanilla extract, and salt and stir until just combined. When it starts to bubble, turn it down to the lowest heat possible and simmer for 3 minutes—do not stir. Be careful because it burns easily!
5. Remove from the heat then whisk in the baking soda. Tip the popcorn into the pot and quickly mix until well coated. Press into the greased baking dish.
6. Place the dark chocolate in a microwave-safe bowl and heat in 30-second intervals, stirring in between, until fully melted. Pour the melted dark chocolate over the top of the popcorn slice, ensuring it is evenly coated. Sprinkle with a generous pinch of sea salt flakes and refrigerate to cool.
7. Once cooled, cut into sixteen pieces with a hot knife. Store in the refrigerator for up to five days in an airtight container.

It is simple and quick to make and tastes delicious! It is also cheap and makes heaps. – Rob

You would never believe this lush chocolate mousse is made using tofu. Simple, smooth, and fluffy, it melts in the mouth and tastes just as decadent as the egg-based version but requires much less effort to prepare. The addition of olive oil takes it to next-level richness.

Chocolate Mousse

TOTAL TIME: 10 MINUTES + 90 MINUTES CHILLING TIME
SERVES 4

7 ounces (200g) plant-based dark chocolate
1 tsp instant coffee
21 ounces (600g) silken tofu, drained
½ cup maple syrup
2 tbsp light olive oil
1 tsp vanilla extract
¼ tsp salt
shaved plant-based dark chocolate to top
Whipped Coconut Cream (page 34) to serve

1. Melt the chocolate and dissolve the instant coffee in a teaspoon of hot water. Put these and the remaining ingredients in a high-powered blender and blitz for 1–2 minutes until smooth and completely combined.
2. Divide the mousse between individual glasses or ramekins, cover, and refrigerate for 90 minutes to firm up.
3. Top with shaved chocolate and serve with Whipped Coconut Cream.

A cookie-base slice (bar) is such a quintessentially Aussie treat to me. Slice was one of the first sweet recipes I learned to make myself, and with no baking required, you can't go wrong. This one is both decadent and nostalgic; the orange flavor is noticeable but not overpowering, and it balances out the sweetness.

Chocolate Orange Slice with Raisins

TOTAL TIME: 45 MINUTES + 90 MINUTES CHILLING TIME
MAKES 12

9 ounces (250g) plant-based cookies such as digestives or tea biscuits
½ cup plant-based butter or margarine
¾ cup plant-based sweetened condensed milk, store bought or homemade (page 32)
1 cup raisins
⅛ tsp salt
1 tbsp finely grated orange zest
1 tsp vanilla extract
3½ ounces (100g) plant-based dark chocolate

1. Line a 8 × 8-inch (20 × 20cm) square baking dish with parchment paper.
2. Crush the cookies in a food processor and pulse for 10 seconds at a time to make a coarse crumb.
3. Place the butter, condensed milk, raisins, and salt in a medium saucepan. Slowly bring to a boil over medium heat. Remove from heat and stir in the grated orange zest and vanilla extract. Add the crushed cookies and mix well. Press the mixture into the lined baking dish.
4. Place the dark chocolate in a microwave-safe bowl and heat in 30-second intervals, stirring in between, until fully melted. Pour the melted dark chocolate over the base and refrigerate for 90 minutes or until set and firm, then slice into twelve pieces. Store in an airtight container in the refrigerator for up to five days.

Something I would be able to make with grandchildren, and it seems to be foolproof. It wasn't too sweet. It was delicious as is but was thinking that adding a little orange liqueur wouldn't hurt. Can't wait for the recipe to be published so I can make a plateful to share with the seniors on game night. – Janet

At the risk of sounding arrogant, these may be the best cookies you've ever tried. They are about 50 percent chocolate, crispy, a little chewy, and very rich.

My recipe calls for chopped dark chocolate—and a lot of it—for a few reasons:

- *Chocolate is delicious.*
- *Chocolate blocks are typically more affordable than vegan chocolate chips.*
- *Chocolate chunks form delicious pools of chocolate in the cookies as they melt, making them extra indulgent.*

You'll also notice that these cookies contain a smidge of instant coffee, but rest assured—they don't taste like coffee. It just brings out a richer flavor from the chocolate.

One-Bowl Chocolate Chunk Cookies

TOTAL TIME: 25 MINUTES
MAKES 12

2 tsp instant coffee
⅓ cup plant-based butter or margarine, chilled
¾ cup brown sugar
½ tsp salt
2 tbsp vegetable oil
1 tsp vanilla extract
1 cup all-purpose flour
1 tsp baking soda
7 ounces (200g) plant-based dark chocolate, chopped
flaky sea salt (optional) to top

1. Preheat the oven to 350°F (180°C). Line a large baking sheet with parchment paper.
2. In a small bowl, dissolve the instant coffee in 1 teaspoon of hot water.
3. In a large mixing bowl, cream the butter, sugar, and salt using an electric mixer until fluffy. Add the oil, vanilla extract, and coffee and keep mixing on low speed until just combined (about 30 seconds). Sift the flour and baking soda into the wet mixture and stir to combine. Add the chopped chocolate and mix again until just combined. If you have time, chill the dough in the fridge for 30 minutes to prevent the cookies from spreading too much.
4. Using your hands, shape the dough into twelve small golf ball–sized balls, or use an ice-cream scoop. Place the balls on the lined baking sheet (do not flatten) and bake for 11 minutes.
5. If desired, sprinkle the baked cookies with flaky sea salt and leave them to cool on the baking sheet for 10 minutes. After 10 minutes they will still be very soft, so use a spatula to gently transfer them to a wire rack to cool completely.

NOTES

Nine times out of ten, I don't bother chilling the dough, but skipping this step means the dough will spread more. The result is a thinner, slightly crispier cookie (I love this!), but technically it is not the ideal cookie from a professional baker viewpoint. That said, chilling the dough is a must if you live in a hot climate, as it will get too soft during mixing.

This recipe calls for a *lot* of chocolate. It may look like too much at first but there is just enough dough to bind it all together. If you want to reduce the amount of chocolate, it's okay—we can still be friends!

Very simple one-bowl, delicious cookies; the coffee adds depth of flavor without being overpowering. – Chapin

The cookies were crispy on the outside and soft on the inside. We also loved the little kick of the coffee flavor. I also sprinkled them with salt when they came out of the oven and they were great! – Ruth

The taste and texture was perfect—they seemed like professional cookies and were some of the best cookies I've ever had (homemade and store bought). Non-vegan family members loved them just as much. – Briana

The batter was so yummy! I would make it just to eat by itself, ha ha. It was also so quick to whip up and cook. It was nice to have a crispy cookie recipe as opposed to a chewy or soft one. – Charlie

There's nothing better than a buttery shortbread cookie dunked in hot tea. This is my Scottish grandmother's recipe that she kindly adapted after my cousin, sister, and I all progressively went vegan. It is very simple, only requires a few ingredients, and makes a big batch.

Easy Classic Shortbread

TOTAL TIME: 45 MINUTES
MAKES 25

3 cups (400g) all-purpose flour
¾ cup (100g) rice flour
1 cup plus 2 tbsp (250g) plant-based butter or margarine
⅔ cup (125g) superfine sugar, plus extra for dusting
½ tsp salt
½ tsp vanilla extract

1. Preheat oven to 350°F (175°C).
2. Sift the flours into a medium bowl.
3. In a large mixing bowl, beat the butter, sugar, salt, and vanilla extract with an electric mixer.
4. Add about half the dry flour mixture to the wet mixture and stir with a spoon until just combined. Add the other half of the flour. Mix with your hands to form a dense and crumbly dough. Bring the dough together by pressing and shaping it with your hands into a large ball.
5. Place the dough on a large sheet of parchment paper that will fit your baking sheet. Use a rolling pin to flatten the dough to ¼–½ inch (1–1½cm) thick in a large rectangular shape. The edges will crack as you roll, so use your hands to gently bring it back together.
6. Carefully slide the parchment paper with the shortbread onto the baking sheet. To create a scalloped edge, firmly press down with your pinky finger around the edges of the dough. Lightly prick the top with a fork in neat rows about ¼ inch (½cm) apart. Use a sharp knife to cut the dough into fingers approximately 3 × 1¼ inches (8 × 3cm), slicing all the way through. Sprinkle with the extra superfine sugar so it is lightly dusted.
7. Bake for 20–25 minutes until it is a very pale gold with slightly darker edges.

NOTES

Shortbread biscuits are dry and crisp. When you combine the ingredients, the dough will appear very crumbly. Don't be tempted to make any adjustments or add liquid, just slowly start shaping the dough into a ball with your hands by firmly pressing it together. The edges will crack as you roll out the dough but keep pushing it back together and it will eventually stay put, I promise. If you find it tricky, try halving the dough and working with two lots instead of one big sheet.

Want to make these even more decadent? Once you have baked the shortbread, let it cool completely, then dip the underside of each in melted dark chocolate. Place them upside down on a drying rack until the chocolate has set.

The shortbread will keep for up to five days in an airtight container or cookie tin. If they taste a little stale, you can refresh them in the oven for 3–5 minutes at 350°F (175°C) to get them nice and crisp again. Only do this once and consume within three days.

This classic hot, syrupy dessert is decadent and warming, the Medjool dates creating a fudgy consistency that binds everything together. Best of all, it requires no unusual ingredients.

Sticky Date Pudding

TOTAL TIME: 1 HOUR 20 MINUTES
SERVES 9

12 Medjool dates, pitted and roughly chopped (about 1 cup)
½ tsp baking soda
1 cup water
1 cup unsweetened plant-based milk
1 tsp vanilla extract
6 tbsp (90g) plant-based butter or margarine
¾ cup brown sugar
1½ cups all-purpose flour
1 tsp baking powder
1 tsp ground cinnamon
½ tsp pumpkin pie spice or mixed spice
¼ tsp salt
plant-based vanilla ice cream to serve

SAUCE
3 tbsp (50g) plant-based butter or margarine
1 cup brown sugar
¼ tsp salt
1 (13.5-ounce/400ml) can coconut cream

1. Preheat the oven to 375°F (190°C). Lightly grease or line a 8 × 8-inch (20 × 20cm) square baking dish.
2. Put the dates, baking soda and water in a large saucepan over medium-high heat, lid on, and bring to a boil. Once boiling, reduce the heat to low and remove lid. Simmer gently for 10 minutes until the dates are soft and almost no liquid remains. Remove from the heat and add the milk, vanilla extract, butter, and sugar. Stir until the sugar is dissolved, then mash the dates into a slurry with some small lumps remaining.
3. Sift the flour, baking powder, cinnamon, spice mix, and salt into a large mixing bowl. Pour the wet mixture into the dry ingredients and stir until just combined. The batter will be thick.
4. Transfer the batter to the prepared baking dish. Bake for 35 minutes or until a skewer inserted comes out clean.
5. While the pudding is baking, make the sauce by combining all the ingredients in a saucepan over medium-high heat. Simmer for 10–15 minutes, stirring occasionally, until the sauce has thickened. Let stand for 5 minutes to thicken further. If separation occurs, whisk before serving.
6. Prick the pudding all over with a fork, then slice into squares. Pour half the sauce over the top and leave to soak for 5 minutes before serving. Serve with a scoop of vanilla ice cream and pour the remaining sauce over the top.

Easily one of my favorite baked goods I've ever made. And I bake a few times a month! This was incredible. Light, so moist, not too sweet (which was surprising! Still sweet but not as sweet as I was expecting) but you get the caramel flavor with that sticky brown sugar and date combo . . . It's absolute perfection. – Courtney

I was first introduced to the magical hot dessert that is cobbler as a teenager at a school friend's house. I immediately loved its syrupy, warming sauce and crusty scone-like topping.

Some cobbler recipes use a soft, cakey topping. I have tried both and I have to say, nothing beats the scone topping for me. It's the perfect contrast of textures paired with the juicy fruit.

Stone Fruit Cobbler

TOTAL TIME: 2 HOURS
SERVES 8

3½ pounds (1.5kg) ripe stone fruit (I like a combination of yellow nectarines, peaches and red plums)
3 tbsp cornstarch
2 tbsp superfine sugar
Whipped Coconut Cream (page 34) or plant-based vanilla ice cream to serve

TOPPING

¾ cup unsweetened plant-based milk
1 tsp vanilla extract
1 tbsp apple cider vinegar
1½ cups all-purpose flour
2 tsp baking powder
½ cup shredded coconut
⅓ cup brown sugar
¼ tsp salt
½ cup plant-based butter or margarine

1. Preheat the oven to 350°F (180°C).
2. Halve the fruit and remove the pits. Slice each half into four slices and place in a large mixing bowl with the cornstarch and superfine sugar, tossing gently to coat. Transfer the fruit to a large 12-cup (3L) capacity baking dish.
3. For the topping, combine the milk, vanilla extract, and vinegar in a small bowl or measuring cup, then leave to rest for 2–3 minutes until thickened and curdled. In a large mixing bowl, sift together the flour and baking powder. Add the coconut, sugar, and salt and whisk to combine. Use your fingers to rub the butter into the dry ingredients until it resembles coarse breadcrumbs. Add the milk mixture and gently mix with a wooden spoon until a dough forms. Dollop the topping onto the stone fruit, leaving some small gaps in between.
4. Place the baking dish on the middle oven rack and a large baking sheet on a lower rack to catch any drips. Bake for 1 hour or until golden.
5. Let stand for 20 minutes before serving to allow the sauce to thicken slightly. Serve with ice cream or Whipped Coconut Cream.

Thank You

This book has truly been a collective effort. I owe a few very special thank-yous to the following people:

My husband, Steve, for lovingly living with my chaos and mess for months.

My parents, David and Fiona, and my sister, Amelia, for always being there to help and encourage me.

My grandmothers, Rena and Norma, for your shortbread and rice pudding recipes.

My host parents, Annie and Dominique, for introducing me to French food and culture.

The professionals: Claire, Miranda, Maria and her team—thank you for sharing your talents with me.

My friends Georgia and James for your professional advice and support. You were involved from the very beginning of this process right through to the end.

My dear friend and creator Sarah Brown, always jumping in to help me cook and create. Your bechamel sauce really made the lasagna recipe.

My friend Theresa, for sharing your mum's amazing koshari recipe.

To Kelly and the team at Affirm Press for the incredible opportunity to create my own book.

And lastly, my biggest thanks of all goes to my recipe testers. Your notes and feedback are woven throughout the book. Whether it be providing substitution options, teaching me the ingredient names in your country, oven temperature variations, flavor adjustments or descriptions, there is a little piece of you on each page. You jumped into recipe-testing in the final weeks before my manuscript was due, when my stress levels were at their highest. Many of you even offered to test multiple recipes. I am so touched by your generosity, kindness and the professional, detailed level of feedback provided. This book would not be the same without you—thank you.

RECIPE TESTERS

Adele Murphy – Adelaide, Australia
Alana Kristapsons – Melbourne, Australia
Alice Billington – Bournemouth, UK
Amelia Douglas – Bundalaguah, Australia
Anna Neubauer – London, UK
Antonia Mertiris – Adelaide, Australia
Ava Mitchell – Melbourne, Australia
Barbara Faucher – Parksville, Canada
Bec Green – Woodend, Australia
Briana Prescott – Christchurch, New Zealand
Bronwyn Ness – Auckland, New Zealand
Caroline Dickenson – Point Leo, Australia
Cathleen M. Hervey – Corpus Christi, USA
Chapin Faulconer – Charlottesville, USA
Charlie Gehrmann – Canberra, Australia
Chloe Douglas – Australia
Christine Lesch – New York, USA
Clare Cartledge – Melbourne, Australia
Claudia Röglsperger – Vienna, Austria
Courtney Barron – Seattle, USA
Cybelle Codish – Detroit, USA
David and Fiona Douglas – Stratford, Australia
Darcie Carruthers – Melbourne, Australia
Dominique Smith – Canada
Elizabeth Roberts – Fountaintown, USA
Eloïse Jennes – Luxembourg, Luxembourg
Erin Brimelow – Naarm, Australia
Erin Logan – Brisbane, Australia
Fiona Sedgwick – Ontario, Canada
Fiona Sorrell – Melbourne, Australia
Georgia Somers-Jones – Melbourne, Australia
Gizem Saruhan – İstanbul, Türkiye
Hannah Cotton – Goulburn, Australia
Jane Patterson – Melbourne, Australia
Janet Tamargo – Austin, USA
Jess Long – Cardiff, UK
Joanne Barrett – Australia
Julia Kroer – Moscow, Russia
Julia Meuter – Berlin, Germany
Julie Cunniffe – Adelaide, Australia
Kaitlyn Labenske – Birmingham, USA
Karen Bassis – Attleboro, USA
Karin Tracy – Los Angeles, USA
Karissa Cornell – Melbourne, Australia
Karolinka van de Werken – Perth, Australia
Kate Huntress – Yarmouth, USA
Kate Olsson – Adelaide, Australia
Katerina Williams – Adelaide, Australia
Katia Massey – Dumfries, UK
Kayla Hellings – Glenreagh, Australia
Kelly McManus – Australia
Kerry Lawrie – Yeppoon, Australia
Kerry Lewry – Singapore
Kerstin Kraasch – Duisburg, Germany
Kim Donaldson – Brisbane, Australia
Larni Jalbert – Brisbane, Australia
Laura Clarke – Toronto, Canada
Lauren Kirkman – Geelong, Australia
Lia Italiano – Nutley, USA
Lisa Felmingham – Melbourne, Australia
Loren Kuppelmeyer – Farmingdale, USA
Lucy McLean – Leeds, UK
Maddie North – Melbourne, Australia
Magdalena Kliszczak – Warsaw, Poland
Mandi Bialek-Wester – Naarm, Australia
Marie B. – Cologne, Germany
Mark & Katie Histon – Sydney, Australia
Marta Benigni – Trento, Italy
Mary Sherwood – Spalding-Lincolnshire, UK
Mary-Ann Johnson – Brisbane, Australia
Matilda Rose Dawson – Melbourne, Australia
Maxine Lockie – Melbourne, Australia
Monica Costa – Melbourne, Australia
Naomi Holmes – Gisborne, Australia
Natalie Snyder – Baltimore, USA
Nuša Števančec – Murska Sobota, Slovenia
Rachel Bass – Albany, Australia
Ragnheidur Olafsdottir – Iceland
Raminta Massey – Brighton, UK
Rebecca Tomlinson – Canterbury, UK
Renelle Trayford – Warrandyte, Australia
Rob Schneider – Adelaide, Australia
Ruth Carda – Minneapolis, USA
Sara Hlin Geirsdottir – Iceland
Sarah Drysdale – Melbourne, Australia
Sarah Gibbs – Lexington, USA
Sarah James – Philadelphia, USA
Selina Jaeck – Sydney, Australia
Sharon Vojtech – Wollongong, Australia
Sheila Savage – Toronto, Canada
Simon Loughran – Somerset, UK
Sue Christensen – Rockhampton, Australia
Sue Cohen – Goulburn, Australia
Sue Szura – Saugatuck, USA
Sumera Subzwari – New York, USA
Summer Healey and Anna Holmes – Brisbane, Australia
Viktoria Kos – Pskov, Russia
Višnja Žugić – Novi Sad, Serbia
Yetsie Loria – Canton, Georgia
Zara Wotherspoon – Melbourne, Australia

Index

Note: page locators in italics denote tips.

A

B

C

D

E

F

G

H

J

K

L

M

N

O

P

Q

R

S

T

V

W

Y

Z